GERMAN SOLDIERS OF WWII

Jean de LAGARDE

Translated from the French by Jean-Pierre VUILLAUME and Alan McKAY

HISTOIRE & COLLECTIONS

CONTENTS

1939

1940

SEAMAN ABOARD THE GRAF SPEE, 1938-39

In the night of 19 to 20 December 1939 after ensuring that his crew was safe, Kapitän zur See Hans Langsdorff, commanding the pocket battleship **Graf Spee** committed suicide in his hotel bedroom in Montevideo, Uruguay. He left a poignant letter explaining his act.

In the morning Oberleutnant zur See H. Dietrich, seconded to Captain Lansgdorff - his orderly had been transferred to the German Embassy in Montevideo - found him on his bed, in white dress uniform and lying on his ship's flag, a bullet hole in the right temple. The tragic death of the last romantic German corsair was the last act in an adventure which started four months earlier at Wilhelmshaven, on 23 August 1939.

The Matrosenobergrefreiter is wearing the sentry duty uniform on the quayside near the Graf Spee's gangway at Wilhelmshaven in the autumn of 1938. He is wearing the navy blue wool cap with tally. The front insignia made up of the golden Navy eagle and national cockade, both made of metal.
The removable collar is made of navy blue cotton, with three white stripes. Under this can be seen the black tie with a thin blue stripe and white braid decorative bow.
The jumper is made of navy blue wool cloth, its sleeves are fastened with two buttons. The Navy eagle is embroidered in golden yellow thread on a navy blue background.

The Navy belt buckle is made of gilt metal. The navy blue wool trousers fave a four-button fly. The pocket side openings are straight. The boots are made of black leather; their leather soles are not hobnailed. Our seaman's weapon is a K98 k.

Matrosenobergrefreiter Schölzel is assigned to one of the 150-mm turrets.
He is connected to the fire direction center by telephone. The cap is made of white cotton cloth. The insignia is of the second type, made in a single piece; the eagle and the cockade are soldered onto a brass plate.
The Reich cockade (black, white and red) was introduced by a decree dated 14 March 1933 replacing the oval cockade bearing the Weimar Republic's eagle in its center. The 24 March 1934 regulation stipulated that the National-Socialist eagle made of yellow metal had to surmount the Reich cockade, the whole being pinned 1/2-inch above the lower limit of the crown. The white cotton jumper has an attached collar.
The blue cuffs with three traditional white stripes are tightened by removable buttons. The breast eagle is embroidered in blue thread on a white background.

SEAMAN ON THE GRAF SPEE, 1938-39

The 21 December 1939 edition of the French news magazine 'Paris-Match' telling the story of the battle between the **Graf Spee** and the British cruisers **Ajax**, **Achilles** and **Exeter** makes up the background of this composition where one can see
the sleeve insignia of Matrosenobergefreiter Schölzel:
– Line crews insignia (**Bootsmannlaufbahn**) embroidered in different materials and background colors according to the type of uniform.
– Double chevron rank insignia of Matrosenobergefreiter.
– Trade badge for single-barreled gun crew chiefs, indicated by the initial 'E' (for **Einzel** = single). These badges with initials were soon to be replaced by others which corresponded to the new trade categories in the Kriegsmarine.
Two sets of insignia are shown as they were placed on the left sleeve, one for the blue jumper (yellow on navy blue background) and the other for the white jumper
(blue on white background).
The breast eagles for these two uniforms are also shown.
Note the thick padded weave and the careful needlework typical of pre-war insignia.

Below.
A collection of petty officer Schölzel's items:
– Blue cap (Mütze) with 'Panzerschiff Graf Spee' tally.
The hat has a name label sewn into the top as stipulated in the regulations.
- White duck trousers with name and service number
(0 1032, drafted in 1937); the aluminum buttons are concave. The trousers were held up by laces pulled in at the waist.
– Seaman's removable collar with white stripes, and white cotton neck flap, intended for wearing with the blue jumper
in full dress.
- Issue sewing needles (Soldaten Nädelbrief).
- Rank chevrons (reverse side) for white smocks with the reception mark (17 May 1939, three months only before the ship left for the South Atlantic).
On the cap tally (left), the text is embroidered with copper thread, typical of pre-war production. After the winter of 1939, this was replaced by yellow thread. The script is German Gothic and the name of the ship is written out in full. This type of tally was replaced after 5 September 1939 by the generic 'Kriegsmarine' tally, for obvious security reasons.

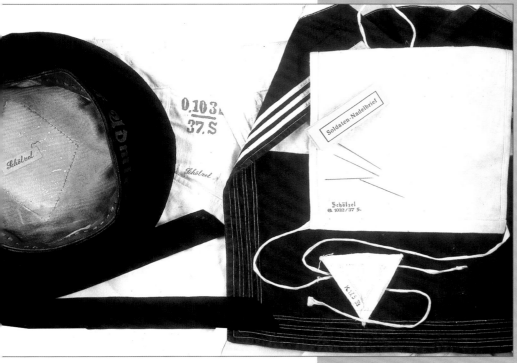

Below.
The Kommandantadmiral's pennant has been hoisted to the mast head to signal his presence aboard. The example illustrated is made of muslin and shows signs of wear and tear. The pennant measures 11 1/2 feet long; at its base
it measures 3 3/4 inches but thins out to
2 1/2 inches at the tip. Eyelets reinforce the edges.
The black Maltese cross is struck on the part closest to the mast.

Graf Spee: Technical Specifications

Type: Pocket battleship (Panzerschiff) launched at Wilhelmshaven on 30 June 1934.
Overall length: 600 feet.
Overall beam: 71 feet 6 inches.
Draught: 16 ft 6 in.
Driven by 8 Diesel engines rated at a total of 54 000 bhp.
Range: about 15 600 miles without refuelling.

Crew: about a thousand men including 44 officers.
Armament: Two 11-in triple turrets, eight single 6-in turrets, three 88-mm double anti-aircraft turrets, eight 37-mm cannon, two quadruple 24-in torpedo launchers, two armed Arado reconnaissance seaplanes.
Mission: Long range surface raider
Results: eleven Allied transports sunk between 30 September 1939 and 7 December 1939, mostly in the South Atlantic.

Opposite page, bottom left.
50 Pfennig aluminum tokens for small expenses in the ship's canteen. In the center, the identification plate for a Kriegsmarine sighting apparatus.

The bosun's whistle with its navy blue cord is made of nickel-plated brass. The name of Matrosenobergefreiter Schölzel has been engraved with a knife.

L'ŒUVRE

FONDATEUR : GUSTAVE TÉRY

N° 8.842. – Lundi 18 décembre 1939.

Le « GRAF SPEE » s'est sabordé à cinq milles de Montevideo

En présence d'une foule qui suivait toutes ses...
le corsaire allemand a le...
à 17 h 15 (heure locale)

Une partie...
avec...

Le Petit Parisien

DERNIÈRE ÉDITION

LE PLUS LU DES JOURNAUX DU MONDE ENTIER

LE "GRAF VON SPEE" AFFRONTERA-T-IL SES ADVERSAIRES ?

La peine de mort au requis EBRA

Se croyant trompé il avait torturé sa femme avant de la tuer

on... ceux qui l'attendent

LE DÉLAI EXPIRERA CE SOIR à 21 h. 30 (G.M.T.)

On this shot clearly inspired by a Signal photograph, Matrosenobergefreiter is here at the top of the gangplank and is using his top man's whistle to indicate the arrival of an officer on board.

On a backdrop made up of French newspapers telling the story of the **Graf Spee** (the Sunday 17 December 1939 edition of **'Le Petit Parisien'** and **'l'Œuvre'** of Monday 18 December 1939) can be seen:

A 37-mm anti-aircraft gun sight, the same type that equipped the pocket battleship Graf Spee. This one was recovered from its sister ship, the **Admiral Scheer**.

A Kriegsmarine thermometer in its wooden box. This standard issue model was for controlling the temperature in the ammunition holds to avoid any risks of explosion.

A Kriegsmarine belt buckle variant, made of anodized aluminum (dated 1938).

A left sleeve trade badge for large caliber gun crews. The embroidered 'T' means **Turm** - turret. The single chevron indicates less than three year's seniority in the trade (two chevrons meant at least three years; three chevrons at least six years). This badge was worn by gunners serving in the two main turrets of the **Graf Spee**, each armed with three 280-mm guns.

A propaganda booklet intended to encourage enlistments in the navy, published in 1939 and open at the page describing the daily P.T. exercises and maintenance work aboard the larger surface vessels.

Zum 0,7 Rf
Nr. 1976

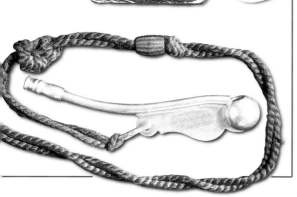

Using a Kriegsmarine dishrag (actually from the Graf Spee) as a backdrop, these are:
- Navy sports shirt eagle, introduced by MV35 dated 3 May 1935. The sports shirt was worn for morning exercise and on duty in hot weather, like on the **Graf Spee** operating in the South Atlantic in the Autumn of 1939.
- Propaganda booklet entitled '**Wie komme ich zur Kriegsmarine**' (How I came to be in the Kriegsmarine) published in 1938 and describing in detail the various careers (**Laufbahnen**) and trades (Sonderausbildungen) of the German Navy.
- An open (cut-throat) razor and its box, an item available in the ship's canteen.
- A white porcelain saucer with the Navy emblem and coming from the **Graf Spee**'s wardroom;
– The generic 'Kriegsmarine' cap tally introduced after the winter of 1939.

CADET OFFICER, 3.PANZER REGIMENT

The Panzer combat badge
This well crafted insignia
is made of embossed gilt metal. It indicates
that the NCO has taken part in three tank
engagements on three different days

Indoors, the corporal is bareheaded
and holds his Schirmmütze peaked cap
under the arm. Like the tunic, the cap
is made of field gray wool cloth,
and adorned with the light metal
eagle and cockade, both high-quality
insignia. The patent leather chinstrap
adjusts with keepers and is secured
with two black buttons on either side.
The crown is piped in pink for tank
troops.
The black belt is fitted with
the Army pebbled aluminum buckle.
The gray trousers are made of
fine, sturdy cloth. The black
pebbled leather shoes have
seven pairs
of eyelets, plain soles
and cleated heels.

Activated in Würzburg in 1935,
the 2nd Panzer Division was commanded by
Colonel Heinz Guderian until
4 February 1938.

The unit was then transferred to Vienna after the
Anschluss. Led by Major-General Rudolf Weiel, the division took part in the Polish campaign in September 1939.
Posted to Romania in April 1941, 2.-Pz. Div. was engaged
in the Balkans and deployed on the Russian front.

This NCO serves with HQ
Company of the 2nd Battalion, 3rd
Armored Regiment. The tailor-made dress
tunic has eight buttons down the front. The
box pleated pockets have scalloped flaps.
The skirt pockets are slightly slanted. The
sleeves have turnback cuffs, and all the
buttons are made of dull grainy metal. The
front is piped in pink, the service color
of the armored forces. The shoulder tabs
are made of bluish-green cloth, piped in pink
and adorned with a figure '3' embroidered
in the service color.
Pink cloth 'Spiegel' (collar tabs) sporting
silver gray 'Litzen' (braid) are sewn on the
collar, which is secured by two hooks and
eyes. The breast eagle is embroidered in
silver gray thread on a dark bluish-green
backing like
the corporal chevrons on the left sleeve.
The man wears the 5th Grade shooting award
for armored units' personnel.
The lanyard is strung between the shoulder
and the tunic's second button down the front.

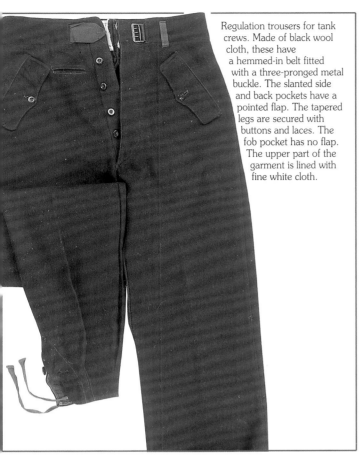

Regulation trousers for tank crews. Made of black wool cloth, these have a hemmed-in belt fitted with a three-pronged metal buckle. The slanted side and back pockets have a pointed flap. The tapered legs are secured with buttons and laces. The fob pocket has no flap. The upper part of the garment is lined with fine white cloth.

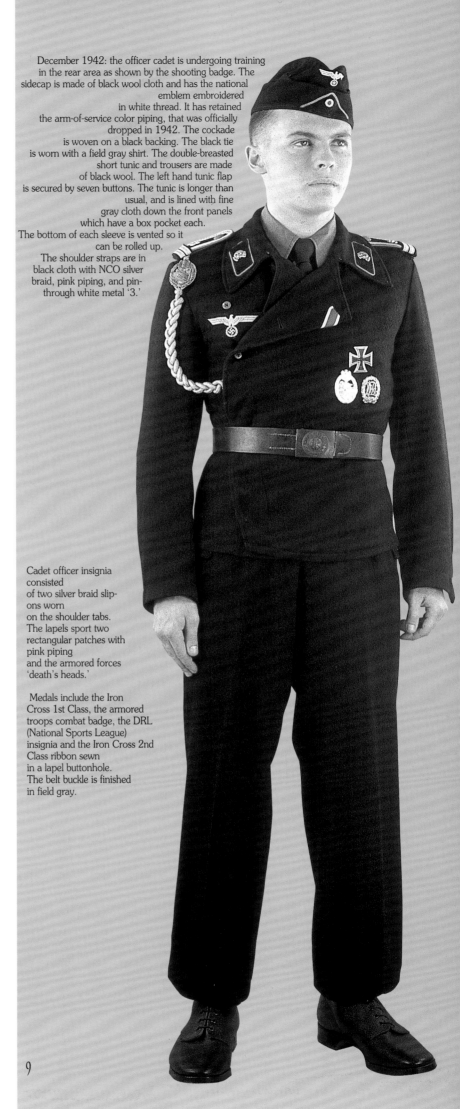

December 1942: the officer cadet is undergoing training in the rear area as shown by the shooting badge. The sidecap is made of black wool cloth and has the national emblem embroidered in white thread. It has retained the arm-of-service color piping, that was officially dropped in 1942. The cockade is woven on a black backing. The black tie is worn with a field gray shirt. The double-breasted short tunic and trousers are made of black wool. The left hand tunic flap is secured by seven buttons. The tunic is longer than usual, and is lined with fine gray cloth down the front panels which have a box pocket each. The bottom of each sleeve is vented so it can be rolled up. The shoulder straps are in black cloth with NCO silver braid, pink piping, and pin-through white metal '3.'

Cadet officer insignia consisted of two silver braid slip-ons worn on the shoulder tabs. The lapels sport two rectangular patches with pink piping and the armored forces 'death's heads.'

Medals include the Iron Cross 1st Class, the armored troops combat badge, the DRL (National Sports League) insignia and the Iron Cross 2nd Class ribbon sewn in a lapel buttonhole. The belt buckle is finished in field gray.

9

INFANTRY SERGEANT, FRANCE, MAY 1940

The uniform is made of unbleached herringbone weave cloth. The tunic has five removable metal buttons down the front, finished in field gray; the collar is secured with a hook. A detachable collar liner in white and field gray cloth protects the neck. The patch pockets have no flaps. A double drawstring gathers the tunic at the waist. The straight trousers are adjusted at the back with a tab and pronged buckle. The fly has five unpainted buttons like those used for the braces. The slash pockets have vertical openings. The patch fob pocket is not visible here. The black leather belt is fitted with a metal buckle. The trousers legs are gathered into black leather jackboots.

After an exhausting campaign, forced marches and brutal engagements, the infantry companies were quartered for a few days.

In the rest areas, the men swapped their field gray wool uniforms for denim fatigues.

During the campaign, this soldier was promoted to sergeant and will soon lead a combat group into action.

The issue sidecap is made of good quality field gray wool. Its metal grommets are finished in olive green. The eagle is woven on a dark green background, and the tricolor cockade on a square piece of dark green cloth. The arm-of-service piping is the infantry white. The chevrons for the fatigue uniform are sewn on the left sleeve. The two corporal chevrons are in light gray braid on a piece of uniform cloth.

The field gray tunic has five buttons down the front. The collar is done up by a metal hook. The collar liner is the same as the one used with the fatigues. The box pleated pockets have three-pointed flaps. The skirt pockets have a side bellows.

The NCO silver-gray braid is sewn around the bluish-green collar. The collar tabs are made of silver-gray thread; the color (white) of the middle strip indicates the branch of service. The collar tabs are sewn on a piece of cloth the same color as the collar.

The shoulder tabs are made of dark blue-green wool material, piped in white and with the silver NCO braid along the edge.

The chest eagle is embroidered in gray thread on a dark green background. The tunic's pebbled metal buttons are finished in field gray.

The NCO is now dressed for battle. The field gray steel helmet sports the national emblem - a transfer - on the left side. The black leather chinstrap is adjusted with a pronged buckle. The issue trousers are in gray wool, and worn with early-war jackboots.

The gas cape oblong pouch is secured on the gas mask strap, slung over the right shoulder. Instead of hanging from the belt on the back, together with the canteen and mess kit, the bread bag is slung over the left shoulder.

INFANTRY SERGEANT, FRANCE, MAY 1940

Below.
The following items
were secured to the belt
so as to be within easy reach
(note: the field gray color
of the grainy belt buckle
has worn off in places)
- A bayonet carried
in a black leather frog,
to which is secured
the NCOs' sword knot
(enhanced with white
and silver braid),
and carried into action
by the man against regulations.
- The black leather wirecutter
carrier.
- The black bakelite field glasses
case. Painted black, the glasses
have 6 x 30 magnification
power.
- One of the two black leather
ammunition pouches for the
Karabiner K98k rifle.
- Below the sidecap,
the black bakelite NCO whistle
was carried
in the right chest pocket
and secured with a thin lanyard
to the tunic's second button
down the front.

Above.
On top of the gray-green canvas
bread bag and its strap, the issue
canteen
and metal cup,
the camouflage 1931-pattern
tent section rolled with black
leather straps placed on top
of the gray-green bread bag; the
gasmask container
and mess tin. The gas cape
protrudes from its pouch
so as to display
the manufacturer's label with
stamped markings indicating
that the item
was issued in 1939.

1941

(© ECPAD/France)

PARATROOPER, CRETE, 1941

The paratrooper wears the airforce field blue side cap adorned with the Luftwaffe gray eagle and national cockade. The water bottle is hooked to a D ring hanging from the belt by a black leather loop. The field gray light gas mask bag is slung over the left shoulder and worn on top of the individual equipment. It is secured to the belt by a metal hook.

The field gray paratrooper trousers are gathered into the jump boots. The vertical pocket has a triangular tab fitted with two pressure studs. It was used to carry the regulation 'gravity knife.' At the back of the smock, the pocket-like added to the right hand side of the skirt can carry a handgun. The rolled up sleeves show the gray cloth lining extending from the wrist to the elbow. This is secured with two buttons in the same way as at the cuffs.

The island of Crete, 20 May 1941. The parachutes of Fallschirmjäger-Regiment 3 blossom in the sky above Hania, one of the island's westernmost towns.

Captain von der Heydte and his men touch down the south of the road leading to Alikianou. Immediately, the Germans become involved in a violent battle with the 15,000 soldiers from the 4th and 10th New Zealand Brigades defending the area.

The corporal's field gray paratrooper helmet sports the Luftwaffe eagle transfer on its left side. The kid leather chin strap is loose and displays its adjustable pressure stud arrangement. The soldier's rank is indicated by two pairs of pressed metal wings superimposed on bright yellow collar tabs (yellow was the flying personnel service color).

The gas mask bag was on exclusive issue to paratroopers. Its flap closes with two studs; the runner of the zipper down the side is fitted with a plastic tab for better grip. The strap adjusts by means of a runner and is secured by a snap hook and buckle. The bag is also secured to the belt by a thick canvas strap fitted with a metal hook. Interestingly, inner reinforcements are made of 'splinter pattern' shelter-half-cloth.

The light green jump smock is made of cotton twill. Its weave reveals a strong proportion of yellowish thread. The garment closes by three blue plastic buttons down the front concealed by a fly, and by two pressure studs near the bottom of the chest pockets. The collar has two pressure studs. The deep upper and skirt slash pockets close with a concealed zipper fitted with a brown leather tab. The lower part of the front and the back of the skirt are fastened together with several sets of pressure studs. Ventilation is provided by vents under the armpits and six eyelets. At waist level vertical slits fitted with concealed zippers grant access to the tunic.
The ammunition pouches for the MP40 submachinegun and a holster for the P08 pistol are slipped onto a brown leather belt secured with an aluminum buckle. A spare magazine sticks out of the right chest pocket.
A hand grenade is carried in the lower pocket. The pressure studs on the cuff have a double socket for a closer fit.
The Luftwaffe emblem is embroidered in white cotton on dark blue wool.

The leather jump boots with 12 eyeholes for side lacing are made of supple, high quality leather, with rubber tread soles.

15

Late April 1941, at night somewhere in the Atlantic: the U-124, a IX-B ocean going submarine, surfaced and steered a westerly course. Commanded by Kapitänleutnant Wilhelm Schultz, the U-124 belonged to the 2nd U-Flotille.

Taking advantage of the darkness, the submarine recharged her batteries as she headed at maximum speed for her pen in Lorien harbor.

The raid had been successful: the U-124 had sunk 11 Allied ships amounting to some 52, 397 tons since she had set sail in February 1941.

For protection against the elements, our seaman has donned a suit of gray oilskins. The suit dark blue collar is kept up by a buttoned strap. The elbows and shoulders are reinforced. The coat's four buttons are covered by a fly front. The pockets have broad flaps and the sleeves have buttoned cuffs. The half belt is fastened by two buttons. In the back, the lower part of the coat has a buttoned vent.

The 'Matrosengefreiter' is about to take the watch in the conning tower where for long hours he will scan the horizon. To ease the strain on his eyes, he wears dark-adaptation goggles with red lenses. His sidecap made of dark blue wool, adorned by an edelweiss on its left side. Initially, this insignia was issued to mountain troops but became the U-124's unofficial emblem. Embroidered in yellow thread, the national eagle is seen above the woven tricolor cockade. The seaman wears a dark blue leather pea-coat over a thick woolen jumper with wide collar. The thick, lined coat has five buttons down the front, all made of dark brown synthetic material. The garment's front and inner pockets have flaps. The cuffs are secured with buttoned straps.

Displayed on a copy of *Die Kriegsmarine*, the German navy's newspaper, are the following items: a navy chest eagle, a diesel engine pressure gauge, a submarine crewman badge and a postcard written on board during the mission.

Made of yellowish material, the life jacket (small type) is firmly secured by two buckled straps. For buoyancy, its flanges are filled with kapok, a rot-proof, watertight material gathered from a tropical tree. The waders are made of dark gray rubber. This sturdy footwear will help to protect the man during his long vigils in the conning tower, as he scans the horizon with his binoculars. The latter's black leather case is slung by a strap over the shoulder.

An hypsometer (or thermo-barometer, used for measuring the height above sea level by observing the boiling point of water with a sensitive thermometer and so therefore determining the relative atmospheric pressure. In the picture, the metal boiler has been attached to the watertight lid. One of the thermometers is on hand to indicate pressure. The receptacles used for collecting sea water are kept in the right part of the case.

17

Displayed on a Kriegsmarine map, this navigation computer is carried in a wooden case. The instrument's classification (MRH 1) is inscribed on a small plate on the inner side of the lid.

Action stations! The Matrosengefreiter has donned his life preserver over his pea-jacket. His steel helmet has the navy blue finish. He is ready to man the 20¾mm anti-aircraft gun which, along a 37 mm and 105 mm gun, make up the U-124's topside armament. The seaman rank badge, a star, is embroidered in yellow thread on a dark blue background. The red trade badge indicates that the man is a hydrophone operator, an important function in a submarine. The badge worn by the 'man with the golden ears' consists of a red arrow embroidered in red thread, thrusting through waves represented in the same way. The backing is an oval piece of dark blue cloth.

A returning U-Boot enter Saint-Nazaire harbor in western France
(Private collectio

Above.

Displayed on a brochure titled 'Wölfe des Meere' (Seawolves), are a training manual (here showing torpedo handling instructions), and a grease gun. On either side of these items are chevrons for leading seamen and the trade badge for hydrophone operators. The blue on white badges (left) were meant for wear with the white canvas rig, and those on the right (yellow/red on blue) with the blue rig.Top, center: Kriegsmarine ID tags, both plain and anodized aluminum.

Right.

The cruise is over. Clean shaved, the Matrosengefreiter is ready to go on leave. At his feet, the sea bag bag holds the personal effects he will take with him. His blue cap has the navy gilt eagle, the national cockade and the 'Kriegsmarine' tally. Lined with gray wool material, the pea-coat is made of thick navy blue cloth. Its five gilt buttons down the front are adorned with an anchor. The collar is done up by a sixth button not seen here. The two inner pockets have flaps. Embroidered in yellow thread, the Kriegsmarine eagle appears on the right hand side of the chest. The lapels bear two plain blue collar patches. The Iron Cross 2nd Class ribbon is slipped and stitched through the top buttonhole, and the submarine crew badge is pinned to the left front. The trousers are made of dark blue cloth, the fly is covered by a flap fastening with four buttons. The pockets have vertical slit openings. The shoes are black leather.

'HEER' ARTILLERY CAPTAIN, EASTERN FRONT, 1941-45

This officer's service cap is made of other ranks' grade wool material. The peak is stiffened and the silver chin strap secured with two gilt buttons. The national cockade and the leaves are embroidered. The eagle is made of embossed metal. The crown piping is bright red.

The officer wears a 1942 Pattern tunic cut in reed green drill material, with a sewn-on dark bluish-green facing cloth collar. The six buttons down the front are finished in field gray. The pocket flaps are pointed. The chest eagle (1937 type) is silver thread embroidered on a dark green backing. The officer's collar tabs consists of rectangular, dark bluish-green patches with silver braid. The bright red strip are in the branch color (artillery bright red). The shoulder straps are edged in the same color, with dull silver braiding. The Iron Cross 1st Class is pinned to the right chest pocket. It was awarded on 24 August 1941, and is worn next to the General assault badge (awarded on 1 August 1941) and the wound badge awarded on 15 August 1942. The officers' belt is made of black leather, and has a pronged buckle finished in field gray.

The breeches are cut in green canvas. The polished jackboots are made of black leather.

Friedrich A. was born in Karlsruhe on 10 May 1919. Commissioned in 1937 with 41st Artillery Regiment (stationed at Ulm). Promoted to captain, he served as an instructor with Assault Gun Training Unit 500.

As a platoon leader on the Eastern front, he destroyed 29 enemy tanks between June 1941 to February 1943. On 20 September 1943, he successfully countered a Soviet thrust in the Jasweno sector, adding a further seven T-34s and one T-60 to his tally. Wounded in this action, he was evacuated a few days later.

On 16¾ November 1943, the lieutenant was awarded the Knight's Cross for conspicuous bravery. At the time, he was commanding the 2nd Section, 2nd Battery of the 237th Assault gun Brigade, deployed on the Eastern Front with Heeresgruppe 'Mitte' (Center), Army Group 'Nord' (North). The Knight's Cross shown here is devoid of manufacturer's markings. Unusually, this superbly crafted medal is finished in black lacquer.

Opposite page, bottom
In October 1942, the officer was awarded the German Cross in Gold for exceptional leadership in action. Manufactured by Deschler of Munich, the medal shown here is made of nickel silver, with gilt wreath, and black and red lacquer. The medal is made up of five parts secured together by four rivets

Promoted to the rank of captain in April 1945, Friedrich A. was awarded the 4th grade General assault badge on 25 March 1945. This award was bestowed on soldiers who had participated in 75 assaults. At the time, the officer was an instructor with the 500th Assault Gun Training Group.

The badge is struck from gray metal. The oval wreath and the '75' figure are gilt finished. The national emblem, the bayonet and stick grenade are in dark gray, and secured with four rivets. This well crafted badge was manufactured by Joseph Feix Söhne, jewelers at Gablonz.

Wounded several times, the officer was awarded the black wound insignia on 15¾August 1942, followed by the silver wound insignia on 16 May 1943 and finally, the gold wound insignia (the highest order, shown here) on 19 September 1943. Made of gilt-finished zinc alloy, the insignia was manufactured by Moritz Hautsch of Pforzheim.

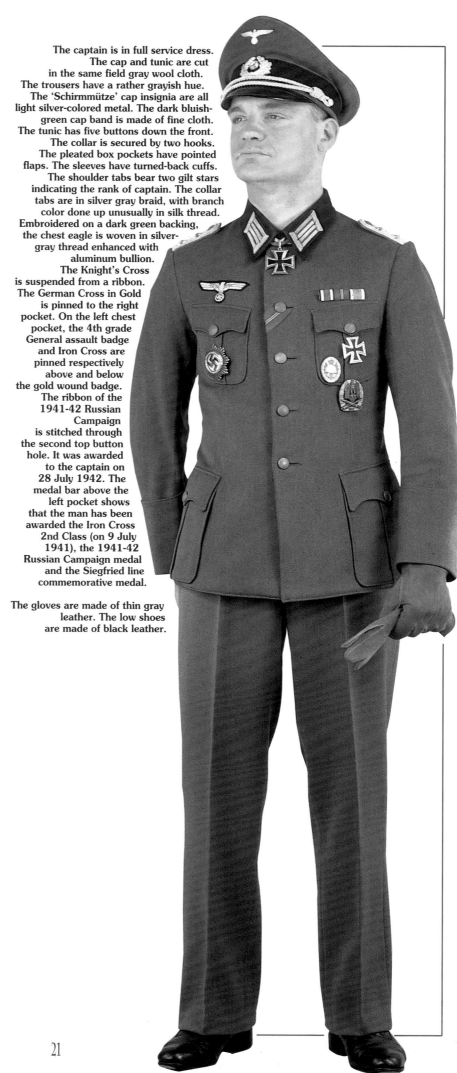

The captain is in full service dress. The cap and tunic are cut in the same field gray wool cloth. The trousers have a rather grayish hue. The 'Schirmmütze' cap insignia are all light silver-colored metal. The dark bluish-green cap band is made of fine cloth. The tunic has five buttons down the front. The collar is secured by two hooks. The pleated box pockets have pointed flaps. The sleeves have turned-back cuffs. The shoulder tabs bear two gilt stars indicating the rank of captain. The collar tabs are in silver gray braid, with branch color done up unusually in silk thread. Embroidered on a dark green backing, the chest eagle is woven in silver-gray thread enhanced with aluminum bullion. The Knight's Cross is suspended from a ribbon. The German Cross in Gold is pinned to the right pocket. On the left chest pocket, the 4th grade General assault badge and Iron Cross are pinned respectively above and below the gold wound badge. The ribbon of the 1941-42 Russian Campaign is stitched through the second top button hole. It was awarded to the captain on 28 July 1942. The medal bar above the left pocket shows that the man has been awarded the Iron Cross 2nd Class (on 9 July 1941), the 1941-42 Russian Campaign medal and the Siegfried line commemorative medal.

The gloves are made of thin gray leather. The low shoes are made of black leather.

194

GEBIRGSJÄGER SUMMER 1942

A sergeant of the 98th Regiment in fighting order. Goggles with tinted lenses are strung around the mountain cap with shortened peak. The 'Windjacke' is worn over the wool service tunic. The shoulder tabs have the NCO silver braid.

On 21 August 1942, elements of the 1st and 4th Gebirgs-Divisions (mountain rifle division) proudly raised their flag on Mount Elbrus (5,633 m) in the Caucasus range. Among the victors were soldiers of the 98th Regiment, 1st Division.

The leather straps of the rucksack are slipped under the shoulder tabs. The ends of the straps are hooked to the MP-40 magazine pouches. Visible above the belt buckle, a black leather strap with pronged buckle keeps the rucksack from swinging around.

Rolled around the bottom of the trousers legs, the puttees are hooked to the leather laces of the mountain boots. Made of steel and wood, the pick was used for climbing.

Made of the same cloth as the tunic, the early type mountain cap with shorter peak has a turn-down with two small buttons. The national emblem is woven in gray thread on a dark green backing. The edelweiss with gold-painted central motif is pinned on the left side. A field gray painted ventilation grommet is set on the crown.

Service tunic for a senior NCO in the 98th Mountain Rifle Regiment
(the light green piped shoulder straps indicate the service branch: mountain infantry).
The collar can be kept up by means of a strap and three buttons.
Also shown are canvas shoulder straps (piped in red for the artillery and yellow
for the reconnaissance group) to be worn with the 'Windjacke' windproof jacket.
Three different types of edelweiss are displayed on the scarf: left, woven
on a bluish-green background; bottom right, woven on uniform cloth backing;
and above right: woven on a field gray backing. German mountain troops
were issued with sleeve and cap edelweiss insignia from May 1939.

Made of cotton, the unlined 'Windjacke' has five buttons down the front.
The cuffs tighten with a button strap. The collar can be kept up by the same
arrangement. The back has a comfort crease and an adjustable buttoned half belt.
Apart from those of the shoulder tabs, all buttons are green synthetic material.
The four pockets have button flaps.

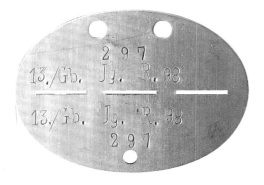

ID tag issued
to a rifleman
of the 13th Company,
98th Regiment
of the 1st Mountain
Rifle Division.

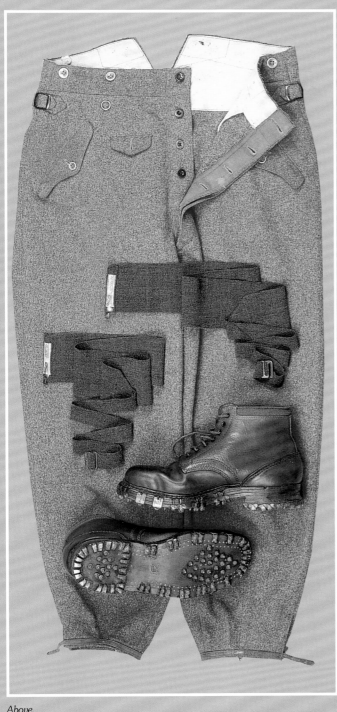

Above.

The mountain trousers. The tapered legs are finished with a strip of a natural leather strip extending into a tightening strap. The trousers have a reinforced seat, and the two front, fob and hip pockets have a button flap. The trousers are kept up with braces and adjust around the waist by means of two straps slipped through a prongless buckle. The buttons are metal or synthetic material. The elastic wool green puttees are secured with hooks and buckles. Their length and the width varies from 1.25 to 1.30 cm and from 8 to 8.5 cm. The mountain shoes have leather laces and seven pairs of eyelets. The upper edge of the boot cuff has a field gray cloth reinforcement. The heel and the thick wooden soles are studded, with crampons around the rim.

The sergeant is clad in a 1942 Pattern field gray tunic with six buttons down the front. The uniform cloth collar and shoulder tabs are adorned with silver gray braid. The chest eagle is woven on a light green background. Sewn on the upper right sleeve, the cloth insignia shows an edelweiss surrounded by a gray rope secured to an eye bolt. The infantry assault badge is pinned next to the left chest pocket.

AFRIKA KORPS INFANTRYMAN

Captured British goggles are carried around the neck.

The pull-over shirt has four synthetic material buttons down the front. The open-collared olive green drill tropical tunic has the Oberschütze (private 1st class) rank insignia on the left sleeve. The infantry assault badge is pinned to the left chest pocket; the Afrika Korps cuff band is sewn onto the bottom of the left sleeve. Standard ammunition pouches made of grainy black leather. The webbing belt is a mint example as indicated by its bright olive green color. The buckle is finished in field gray. A 1924 Pattern stick grenade has been stuck under the belt.

Web anklets with leather straps and lower edge reinforcements.

QUITE typical of the German soldier fighting at El Alamein, this Oberschütze belongs to the 21st Panzer Division's 104th Panzergrenadier Regiment.

Individual equipment: the pattern 1931 olive green bread bag is fastened to the belt with two buttoned straps and a flat hook. The two tropical water bottles are made of aluminum, covered with a mixture of vulcanized fibre and wood. The strap securing the bakelite cup is slipped through a strap on the bag flap. The entrenching tool carrier is a locally-made variant. Its bottom strap also secures the bayonet scabbard. The standard 84/98 Pattern bayonet is carried in its own webbing frog.

Opposite page.
The cotton twill trousers are fastened with a belt fitted with a painted metal buckle. There is a fourth flapped pocket on the right hip. The braces button onto the two short vertical tabs at the back. The pockets have a gray lining. The trousers are straight-legged, with no tightening straps. The leather and canvas tropical shoes bear 48-50 hobnails on the sole and a typical U-shaped cleat on the heel. The manufacturer's name is stamped on the tongue of the boot; the production year is etched on the sole.

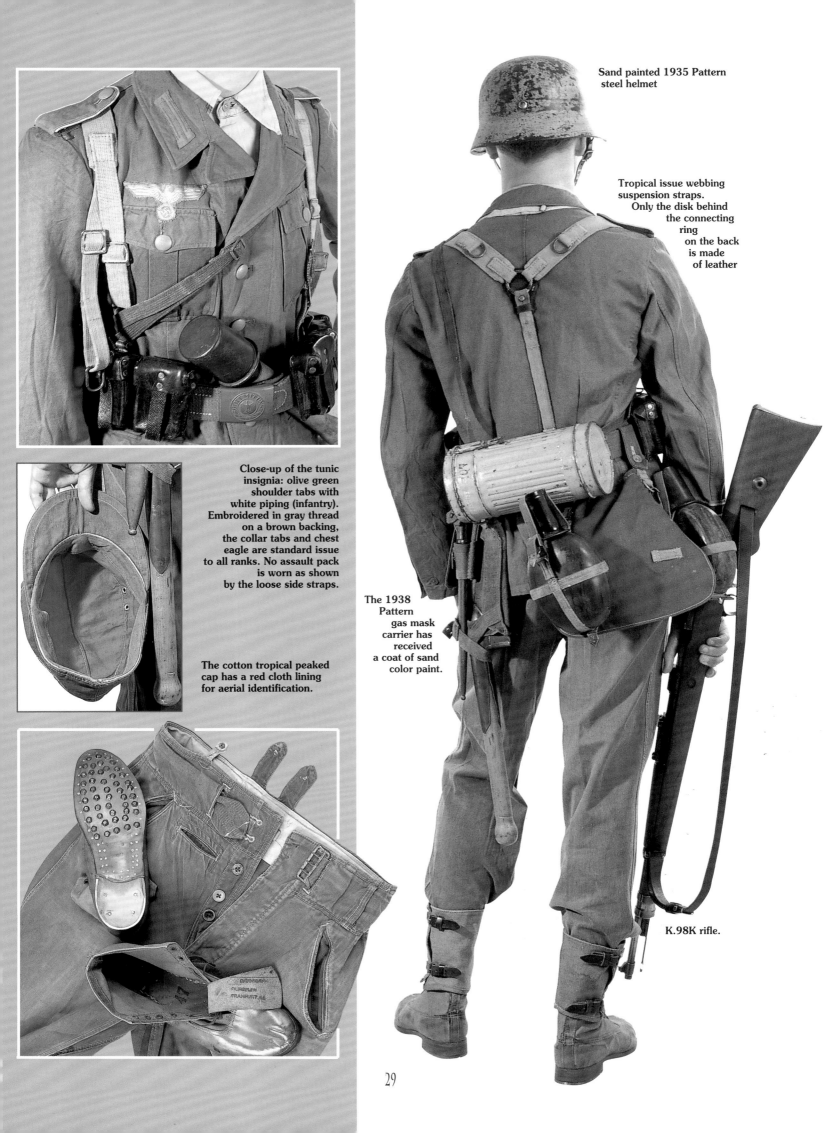

Sand painted 1935 Pattern steel helmet

Tropical issue webbing suspension straps. Only the disk behind the connecting ring on the back is made of leather

Close-up of the tunic insignia: olive green shoulder tabs with white piping (infantry). Embroidered in gray thread on a brown backing, the collar tabs and chest eagle are standard issue to all ranks. No assault pack is worn as shown by the loose side straps.

The cotton tropical peaked cap has a red cloth lining for aerial identification.

The 1938 Pattern gas mask carrier has received a coat of sand color paint.

K.98K rifle.

29

INFANTRYMAN ON SUPPLY DUTY

The greatcoat is made of field gray cloth. Lined with gray material, it has a double row of six buttons down the front. The collar is done up with a hook and eyelet arrangement. The slanted pockets have broad flaps. The cuffs have turn-ups. Piped in white (the infantry service color), the field gray shoulder straps are secured by a tab at the sleeve and a button near the collar. The knit gloves are gray.

Night falls over the battlefield. The front line goes quiet after a long day's struggle through the snow and mud.

Soon, shadowy figures will sneak towards the assault group clinging to the hard won ground. In the bleak landscape lit only by the wrecks of the burning tanks, soldiers on supply duty will selflessly deliver hot rations to their comrades. Further back, the division's bakers and butchers will have a busy time working over hot stoves until dawn.

The ammo pouches for the Kar 98 K rifle are made of black leather, like the belt fastened with a field gray painted buckle.
The 'Heer' private carries a large spoon and four field gray painted mess tins (mess tins were available in several shades, glossy and matt).

Painted green, the aluminum food container has a round screw top. It is secured to a black-painted metal frame. The carrying straps crisscrossing over the back are made of tan web. They are adjusted with a pronged buckle at kidney level and secure to the front strap. The load is held in place by three horizontal and one vertical strap fitted with steel buckles.

For improved camouflage, the helmet has been daubed with a mixture of tan paint and sand. The green-painted food container has a handle fitted to its lid. Strung around the man's neck are several water bottles (the various colors of the cups are noteworthy). The reversible white parka is worn here with its mouse gray side out. This warm garment is made of thick cotton. Lined with wool (apart from the hood), the garment has six metal buttons down the front fitting into double buttonholes.

The inner pockets have a large slanted button flap. Like the hood, the parka adjusts with a drawstring along its edge. The cuffs have buttons for tightening. The waist is gathered thanks to sliding tape.

The trousers are made of thick field gray cloth, gathered into black leather high boots worn as a protection against extreme weather conditions. The shaft is made of thick black felt, the soles are studded and the heels cleated.

1. Aluminum jug.
2. Bakelite salt box with sliding lid.
3. Aluminum coffee container with hinged lid and carrying handle.
4. Aluminum pepper box. The screw top is tied with a steel chain.
5. Portable Esbit cooker. Made of steel, and supplied in a cardboard container, it is shown here with heating tablets.
6. Box of matches with protective cover.
7. Folding set of eating utensils combining a fork and a spoon.
8. Two of the four eating utensil sets with built-in tin openers.
9. Glass brandy bottle in wooden container with swiveling lid for expedition through the Army postal service.
10. Tinned chocolate.
11. Bread in paper wrapper.
12. Paper bag containing seasoning for hot meals (soup and meat).
13. Powdered egg bags.
14. Bag of seasoning.
15. Bag of juniper berries for cooking pork dishes.

U-BOAT KAPITÄNLEUTNANT

SUMMER 1942, somewhere in the Atlantic off the French coast. Her mission over, a submarine is heading back to her pen.

On board, the men are exhausted; constantly dodging escort destroyers, diving to escape depth charges, unceasing watches and alternating from being the hunter to the hunted is taking its toll. But soon, the 'gray wolf' will be back to the safety of Brest harbor.

When the weather allowed, this light uniform could be worn on deck duties as shown by the man's 7 x 50 navy binoculars. The short jacket's five front buttons are made of black synthetic material. The pleated chest pockets have pointed flaps. The waist adjusts by means of a metal buckle and strap arrangement. The cuffs are plain with a single button. The chest eagle is made of stamped gilt metal. It is secured by a pin slipped through thread loops stitched on the garment.

The baggy drill trousers have two flap less pockets. They are done up by a button strap at the front. The ankles are gathered together with three dished metal buttons (smaller pattern).

Standard army boots.

Above.
Navy officer's sidecap with unofficial ship badge, 7 x 50 binoculars, sextant with white Kriegsmarine property mark (an eagle and a gothic letter 'M').

Made of dark blue cloth, the sidecap is piped with aluminum braid for officers. The eagle is embroidered in gray thread and the cockade is standard issue. The silvered brass swordfish - the emblem of the 9 U-Flotille - is secured to the left side by two flat pins. The shoulder straps for a Kapitänleutnant consist of silver braid adorned with two gilt stars on a dark blue backing. The straps are secured by loops near the armhole and buttons near the collar. The gilt buttons bear the Kriegsmarine anchor.

Back ashore, and now clean-shaven, the U-boat captain has recovered from his eventful journey. His walking out uniform consists of a 'Schirmmütze' peaked cap, a double-breasted tunic of fine blue wool and matching trousers. The tunic has a double row of gilt navy pattern buttons down the front. The hip pockets have horizontal slits with rectangular flaps. A small flap less pocket is set above the fifth button from the left. The rank stripes are sewn 11.5 cm from the sleeve edge, the middle one being slightly narrower. The stripes are made of gilt-finished aluminum braid, like the five-pointed star badge of line (seagoing) personnel. The Iron Cross 2d class ribbon is slipped through the fourth buttonhole. On the left side, the officer sports the Iron Cross 1st class and the badge awardedto submarine crews after two run-ins with the enemy. A white cotton shirt and a black tie complete the uniform. The fine serge blue trousers have optional turn-ups. The shoes are made of black leather. The trousers are kept up by braces. The hip pockets are straight, and the hip pocket has a button flap. The trousers are adjusted with buckle straps on the hips. All buttons are made of black synthetic material.

The ceremonial dagger is worn on the left hand side, with the hangers slipped under the tunic.

The cap issued to Kriegsmarine officers was made of fine blue cloth. The eagle and the oak leaves are embroidered of golden bullion. The patent leather chin strap is fastened by two gilt anchor buttons (smaller pattern). An embroidered gilt scalloped braid runs around the edge of the peak. The navy officer's dagger has a brass scabbard, guard and pommel. The handle has a wooden core covered in a plastic-like material. The scabbard is decorated with engravings representing bolts of lighting. The pommel is an eagle with half folded wings. The knot is looped around the scabbard as per regulations. The black ribbon hangers are affixed to a gold-colored lion head buckle and snap fastener. The upper hanger has a small ring with a chain for hooking up the dagger. Protected by a mica cover, the Navy commanding officer's car pennant consists of an eagle embroidered in yellow thread on a dark blue backing.

SENTRY IN WINTER CLOTHING

A hood of thick white cloth covers the helmet. The collar of the overcoat has been turned up to protect the sentry's face; it is kept up by the stiffness of the cloth and fastened with a button and strap arrangement.

Guarding the command post of the armored group's CO, the 'Schütze' has donned a thick overcoat over his greatcoat and uniform. Apart from the sleeves, this overcoat is fully lined with white sheepskin and cut in thick gray cloth. Reaching down to the ankles, the double-breasted garment has two rows of field gray buttons down the front. The chest and side pockets have respectively vertical and horizontal openings, and the latter, buttoned flaps. The half belt on the back is fastened with two buttons. The skirt vent in the back has a flap secured with four buttons made of green synthetic material.

The unit commander gave the order to stop. Immediately, the column of tanks and half tracks ground to a halt by the edge of the snowbound forest.

The tanks and APCs positioned themselves into a defen[s]ive screen for the soft-skinned vehicles and trucks. Completely exha[ust]ed, the men tried to snatch some sleep on the frozen grou[nd]. During their rest, the troops were protected by the unsung he[roes] whose courage and dedication have never received the praise [they] deserve: the sentries.

Winter 1941-42. The 1935 Pattern steel helmet is finished in glossy dark gray. The black shield-shaped decal on the left side is adorned with the silver Wehrmacht eagle. Made of thick white cloth, the hood is folded back over the shoulders. The field gray shoulder straps are piped in pink, the armored troops color. The straps are buttoned near the collar and secured at the shoulder seam by a loop. The tube-like, stretchable wool scarf/headcover protects the face from the nose down.

Left.
For better insulation, the sentry has donned thick felt boots over his black leather regulation jackboots. The wool-lined field gray mittens are worn over the issue woolen gra[y] knit gloves. The sentry is armed with a PPSH 41 submachine-gun captured from the Soviets.

Opposite page, bottom le[ft]
Respectively 3 and 4 cm thick, the soles and heels of the overboo[ts] are made of black painted wood. The felt shaft is 1 cm thick an[d] reinforced with a thin black leather strip. The two brown straps ar[e] fitted with a pronged metal buckle. The high winter boots worn b[y] the soldier on the right have a gray felt shaft fastening at the bac[k] with a strap and pronged buckle. The uppers are made of blac[k] leather witha brown stiffening. The leather soles are secured wit[h] wooden pegs. The leather reinforcing and non-skid patches on th[e] [sole]zsoles are affixed with steel nail[s]

The anti-glare goggles have an aluminum frame and yellow-tinted lenses.

Winter 1942-43.
The 'Schütze's helmet has a white cotton cover. Made up of five pieces, it is fastened with a drawstring around the rim. Worn over the thick wool greatcoat, the white smock is made of flimsy cotton and has three buttons down the front. Access to the greatcoat's pockets is granted through two slanted slits. The hood is wide enough to accommodate the helmet. The smock is gathered around the waist by a regulation black leather belt fitted with a field gray buckle.

This inside view of the fur lined overcoat (far left) shows the vertical slits opening for the inner left pocket in the front. The large cloth hood in the wide turn up collar is clearly shown. It covers the helmet when worn.

A wool knit glove (large size as indicated by the three white rings around the wrist), a field gray mitten and a gray felt mitten are displayed on the white smock. The smock buttons and the hip openings for access to the greatcoat's pockets are clearly shown.

35

1943

Outfitted in the motorcycle rider's special uniform, the NCO is about to take his place in a sidecar for traffic directing duties in the operational zone

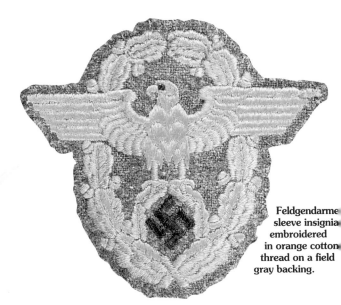

Feldgendarme sleeve insignia embroidered in orange cotton thread on a field gray backing.

The MP 40 submachine-gun magazine pouch and the map case are secured to the right and left sides of the leather belt. The gasmask carrier - to which the gas cape pouch is strapped - is slung around the neck. The gray suede gloves are regulation issue for senior NCOs and officers. The protective coat and goggles were issued only to motorcyclists. The collar of the rubberized fabric coat is faced with field gray wool. The collar can be worn turned up thanks to a strap and button arrangement. The pocket flaps have one button and the cuffs two. The garment is done up at right hip level with buttons. There is a vertical, flapless pocket on the right side of the chest. A yoke with a vertical vent covers the shoulders. The bottom vent of the garment can be done up with four buttons.

Originally raised from the ranks of the civilian uniformed police, the Feldgendarmerie was a subunit of the army's provost corps.

In addition to keeping law and order among the troops, the Feldgendarmes' missions included gathering prisoners of war and refugees, protecting captured equipment, controlling the population in occupied territories and directing traffic.

Above.
Woven in brown cotton thread, the cuff title at the bottom of the sleeve has gray stripes and Gothic letters. The shoulder tabs, with dark greenish-blue backing, are piped with orange around
the edge. Two metallic hooks are secured to the back of the gorget: one is used to hold the chain while the other is slipped into one of the tunic buttonholes. The back of the gorget is covered in feldgrau cloth to reduce wear.

The senior NCO is checking identity documents. His steel helmet is a 1935/42 pattern with the Army decal on the left side. Two regulation insignia are worn on the 1942-43 Pattern tunic: the sleeve badge and the cuff title. The officer has been awarded the medal for the 1941-42 Winter Campaign in addition to the National Sports award pinned to the left pocket. The holster for the P38 pistol is worn on the left hip in compliance with regulations.

The 'Feldgendarme's' gorget plate is secured to the Oberfeldwebel's tunic. The gorget is made of light pressed metal and finished in silver. Its chain has 42 links. The eagle, buttons and 'Feldgendarmerie' inscription on a dark gray scroll are coated in fluorescent yellow paint. These four components are secured to the gorget plate by hooks. The typical field police badge on the sleeve is embroidered in orange, the arm-of-service color.

HAUPTWACHTMEISTER, MARSEILLE

The tunic of the Schutzpolizei senior NCO is made of Police green cloth. The garment is done up by means of two hooks (collar) and eight metal buttons down the front. The left hand front panel has the light green branch piping. The pleated chest pockets and the lower patch pockets have three-pointed flaps. Like the collar, the cuff turn ups are made of brown facing cloth, piped in green and adorned with two buttons.

The embossed metal buttons are finished in dull aluminum (only those of the shoulder tabs are smaller).

The DLR (Deutsche Reichsbund for Leibesübungen - German Gymnastics Association) award is pinned to the left chest pocket.

The serge trousers are matching the tunic. They are worn with black leather jackboots.

The holster for the P.08 is worn on the right hand side. Strung over the right shoulder, the cross strap connects to the black leather belt by means of a snap hook (adjusted with a prong less buckle).

The two silver stars of 'Haupt-wachtmeister' appear on the shoulder straps. These feature green and interwoven silver/brown braiding, with a light green piping around the edge.

Early in 1943, the Germans decided to demolish the backstreet area around the 'Vieux port' in Marseilles. Provisional 'Polizei-Regiment Griese,' from the name of its commander, which had been established recently in Southern France, was tasked with searching and evacuating this squalid neighborhood.

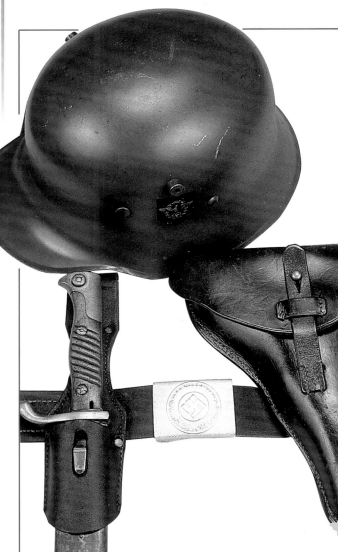

On the left side of the helmet (originally an Austrian 1916 Pattern), the transfer insignia is the Polizei silver eagle on a black shield. The ¾grainy aluminum belt buckle features a swastika surrounded by a wreath and carries the 'Gott Mit uns' (God with us) motto in its upper portion. The black holster for the P.08 handgun is police standard issue, as shown by the short strap and stud closure. The bayonet is the standard 98/05 Mauser model.

Above.
Made of black grainy leather, the ammo pouches are carried on the leather belt with aluminum buckle.

Below.
The sidecap is made of green cloth and has one field gray ventilation grummet on one side. The Police type national insignia, sewn on the front, is woven in white thread on a black background. Piped in green, the tunic collar is made of fine brown cloth. The collar tabs are made of light green cloth with silver gray 'tresse.' Embroidered in light green thread on a dark green backing, the Police eagle is worn on the left sleeve.

The NCO is armed with a 98A Mauser carbine fitted with a brown leather sling. The straps slung across the chest are for the bread bag and gasmask carrier. The greatcoat is cut from thick green wool material and lined with dark gray cloth. It is double-breasted with two rows of six silver-finish aluminum buttons. The wide collar, in brown material piped in green, closes by a hook and eye. The side pockets are slanted and covered with a ¾ wide flap.

Issue gray knit gloves

Below.
Close up of the field equipment: gas mask carrier, green canvas bread bag, mess kit and water bottle. The bayonet frog is positioned on the left side.

'DEUTSCHLAND' SQUAD LEADER

Secured by a tab and a button, the white piped shoulder straps are made of black cloth. They bear the regiment's initial, a gothic 'D', along with two silver rank stars. The silver braid of 'Hauptscharführer' (senior NCO) is sewn on the edge of the straps and around the tunic collar. The right collar tab is adorned with the SS runes embroidered in silver-gray thread. On the left patch, rank is indicated by two silver stars and stripes. The eagle insignia on the left arm is woven in silver gray thread on a black backing. The Iron Cross 1st Class and the infantry assault badge are pinned to the left pocket. Two medal ribbons (Iron Cross 2d Class and 1941-42 Russian Campaign) are slipped through the second buttonhole down the front. Carried in the right chest pocket, the NCO whistle is secured with a lanyard to the tunic's second buttonhole. The black leather belt is fitted with the typical SS pressed metal buckle. The P-38 holster is carried on the belt.

LATE on 9 May 1943, Obergruppenführer Paul Hausser, commander of the SS-Panzerkorps in Russia, outlined his plan for the reconquest of Kharkov which his troops has evacuated a few weeks previously.

The commander of the 'Totenkopf' Division was ordered to skirt the city and hold its northern sector while the 'Leibstandarte' would attack from the west. The men of 'Das Reich' were briefed to thrust from the east and seize the main railway station. On 12 March, the station fell to the Germans after a spirited defense which forced the grudging admiration of the victors. However it would take another two days of bitter struggle in the mud and snow before the SS wrested the gutted city back from the gallant Red Army.

The Waffen-SS sidecap is made of field gray cloth. The insignia at the front, a death's head topped with an eagle, are woven in gray thread on a black backing. Worn over a gray jersey shirt, the tunic is done up with five buttons down the front and a steel hook at the collar. The garment has four pockets - the lower ones are pleated - with scalloped flaps.

The steel helmet has been coated with white paint. Its chin strap is made of black leather and secured with a pronged buckle. For protection against the cold, the NCO wears a scarf of fine field gray wool in addition to his thick field gray padded parka.

The parka is done up with eight buttons. Made of metal and painted field gray, they are covered by a narrow flap down the front. The garment has patch pockets on the chest and inside-hanging pockets on the skirt. All the pockets have a pointed flap. The deep skirt pockets are lined with wool and thick sheepskin. The parka is lined with brown sheep wool; the sleeves are padded with wool scraps and waste. The cuffs are gathered by an elasticated band. The waist is fastened by a hemmed in, non-adjustable elasticated band.

The 'Soldbuch' (paybook) was carried in one of the tunic's chest pockets. Inside the book, the man's picture (in uniform) is secured with two staples. Sewn 14.5 cm above the sleeve edge of the service tunic, the cuff title is made of black braid with two aluminum thread stripes. The gothic lettering is woven in silver-gray thread.

Bottom right.
Waffen-SS other ranks pressed aluminum belt ¾buckle.

SS

Soldbuch

zugleich

Personalausweis

Deutschland

43

POLIZEI BATTALION, THE SOVIET UNION

The policeman is shown here clad in the field uniform he wore in action throughout summer 1943. Polizei units were heavily committed in the Briansk forests and the Pripet marshes.

The shoulder straps of 'Unterwachmeister' are made of a fine green cloth backing with a 'U'-shaped central strip. The edge is made of the same material but enhanced with a silver-gray threaded pattern.
The 'Schutzpolizei' eagle insignia is sewn on the left sleeve. It is woven in light green thread on a fine green cloth backing and features a black swastika on a light green oak leaf packing.

Black leather belt with embossed aluminum buckle, grainy leather ammo pouches. The individual weapon is the K-98k rifle.

In the same color as the tunic, the trousers are tucked into the black boots.

Right.
The tunic is displayed to show the field dressing pocket in the inner front of the garment. The field dressing is marked 'Polizei-Sanitätslager-Berlin NW40.' The pocket and lining are cut from the same pale green cloth. The inner tabs securing the belt hooks have five oversewn eyelets. The tunic has no inside pocket. The white cloth label indicates that the water bottle belongs to a policeman.

WHEN the German army swept through the Soviet Union in 1941 large numbers of Russia soldiers were cut off. Soon, these regulars were joined by partisans and, by 1942, they had formed into organised underground brigades. Led by unconventional warfare specialists, they raided communication and supply lines in the Wehrmacht's' rear. Repression was ruthless.
The Germans carried out massive search and destroy operations, particularly in spring 1943 when more than 60,000 soldiers took part in a massive sweep in the forests between Briansk and Gomel. The subject of this close-up is a member of a 'Schutzpolizei' unit as he appeared during this action.

Earlier in the war, our policeman is pictured in front of a poster celebrating the 1941 'German Police Day,' a charity event at the onset of winter. The man wears a 1935 Pattern steel helmet. Finished in glossy field gray, this sports two transfers: on the left, the red shield with the white disk and swastika, and on the right, the silver police eagle on a black shield. The black leather chin strap has a pronged buckle. The policeman's tunic - manufactured in 1940 - is made of fine wool serge intended for the warm seasons. Its greenish hue is typical of Police issue uniforms.

The edge of the left panel is piped in green, the branch color. The pleated chest pockets and skirt patch pockets have three pointed button flaps. Piped in green and adorned with two buttons, the cuff turn-ups are in brown cloth. A vent adorned with two buttons, and green piped facings runs down the lower part of the tunic.

Made of fine brown cloth, the collar is piped in green and secured with two hooks. Cut in fine green material, the collar patches have dull silver 'tresse' and edging. They are piped in the arm-of-service color. The bronze SA Military Sports badge is worn on the left chest pocket.

Right.
Displayed on a March 1942 German Police Force periodical are the following items: a postcard sold by the police and the SS on behalf of the 1942 winter relief; an aluminum badge featuring the police insignia and commemorating the 1942 Police Celebration Day and, finally, a police association lapel badge.

'HERMANN GÖRING' PANZERGRENADIER

The black tie is worn over a shirt of fine blue cloth. The 'Fliegerbluse' is cut in regulation blue-gray cloth. The fly-fronted, double breasted garment is done up by five buttons (larger pattern) down the front. The collar has a hook and eye.

The ribbon of the Iron Cross 2nd Class is slipped through the third blouse buttonhole. The blue ribbon adorned with silver eagle was awarded for four years' service. The Iron Cross 1st Class is pinned above the Luftwaffe assault badge. This Condor Legion veteran wears the prestigious Spanish Cross with Swords on the right side of the chest.

The P-08 holster is slipped on the black leather belt fitted with a Luftwaffe regulation buckle. Matching the blouse, the straight trousers are tucked into black leather boots.

In late August 1943, veterans of the 'Hermann Göring' Armored Division were mustered at Caserta to the north of Naples for refitting after the hard-fought Sicily campaign.

Reinforcements had been brought in from France so that General Conrath could bolster his unit before meeting the Allies who were to land at Salerno during the night of 8-9 September. Conrath's force was already understrength when it was committed at dawn on 9 September. In the evening, a German company encountered the enemy on Mount San Angelo. Under massive shelling by British and American warships, the 'Hermann Göring' divisional recce group headed for Maiori which was already held by American rangers. The hills were rocked with explosions as throughout the day attack followed counter-attack before eventually petering out into hand-to-hand fighting. But their efforts were to no avail and the men of the elite Luftwaffe division laid down their lives in vain: by nightfall, more than 50,000 British and American soldiers had set foot on Italian soil.

The Luftwaffe shooting badge (first grade) is strung between the second blouse button and the right shoulder strap. The ¾ award consists of an oval badge secured to a twisted cord covered with a pattern of blue-gray and aluminum thread. The badge features a silver eagle and oak leaves. The shoulder straps are made of blue-gray cloth, piped in white, edged with dull silver NCO braiding (also visible on the collar edge) and with a single rank star. The white collar tabs are adorned with three stylized metal wings.

Stamped on the inner left pocket of the blouse, the regulation markings include the following (from top to bottom): 41 (torso measurement), 67 (length), 96 (waist). The breadth across the shoulders has been erased. The manufacturer's stamp (W. Drews-Sohn) is followed by three letters: 'LBA' (Luftwaffe Bekleidungs Amt - Luftwaffe clothing depot), and by the figure '39' indicating the year in which the tunic was made. The unit stamp reads 'II ERS. BATL - RG - HG' (2nd depot battalion of the H. Göring Regiment). The belt buckle leather tab also has 'II REGT. GEN. GÖRING. The regiment was expanded to brigade strength in July 1942 before becoming the 'Hermann Göring Division' on 15 October. The unit was raised to Panzer Division status in May 1943.

Below.

Issued to other-ranks and NCOs, the cuff title is made of a dark blue cloth strip with lettering embroidered in silver-gray thread.

This other rank pattern 'Schirmmütze' (peaked cap) is cut in blue-gray cloth and has a black band. The black patent peak has a stitched oilcloth binding. Held in place by two black buttons, the black leather chin strap has two buckles at the front and one flat keeper on each side. The arm of service piping is white. Secured to the front of the cap, the Luftwaffe eagle and the winged cockade are made of embossed silver metal.

The main component of the 'Spanienkreuz' award is a Maltese cross. The first German campaign medal, the cross is unusually large (54-57 mm) and was worn on the right side of the chest. The 'Spanienkreuz' shown here is made of nickel silver, with a swastika which protrudes more than on other variants. The swords and eagles are particularly well finished. L.52, the trademark of manufacturer Gottlieb Wagner, is etched on the cross.

The Waffen-SS camouflage garments worn by the NCO (helmet cover and smock) have the same camouflage pattern of dark brown, brown, dark green and green intermingled blotches. The early type smock has an opening for the head extending into a front slit running down to mid chest, and done up with a lace strung through five pairs of oversewn eyelets. The elasticated bands on the cuffs have slackened with age. The smock skirt is tucked up into the belt. The belt carrying the ammo pouches (three MP-40 submachine-gun magazines) is held up by black leather suspension straps.

FIGHTER PILOT, SICILY

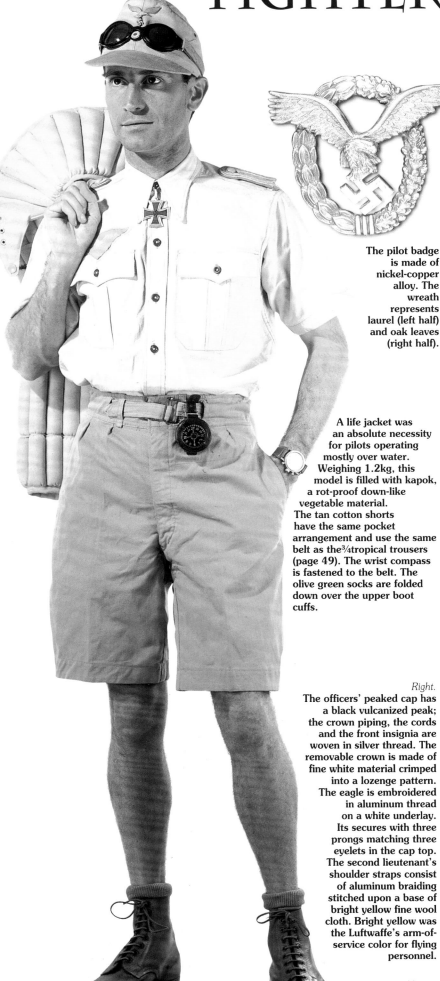

The pilot badge is made of nickel-copper alloy. The wreath represents laurel (left half) and oak leaves (right half).

A life jacket was an absolute necessity for pilots operating mostly over water. Weighing 1.2kg, this model is filled with kapok, a rot-proof down-like vegetable material. The tan cotton shorts have the same pocket arrangement and use the same belt as the ¾tropical trousers (page 49). The wrist compass is fastened to the belt. The olive green socks are folded down over the upper boot cuffs.

Right.
The officers' peaked cap has a black vulcanized peak; the crown piping, the cords and the front insignia are woven in silver thread. The removable crown is made of fine white material crimped into a lozenge pattern. The eagle is embroidered in aluminum thread on a white underlay. Its secures with three prongs matching three eyelets in the cap top. The second lieutenant's shoulder straps consist of aluminum braiding stitched upon a base of bright yellow fine wool cloth. Bright yellow was the Luftwaffe's arm-of-service color for flying personnel.

THE 3rd Group of 26th Heavy Fighter Squadron was deployed in the Mediterranean shortly after the Western desert campaign ended. The unit fought there for 30 months, notching up 130 enemy aircraft and 1,210 armored and soft-skinned vehicles for the loss of 252 crewmen.

Opposite page, top
Cut in tan cotton, the officer's field cap has two brown finished ventilation grommets on either side. The front of the cap is adorned by a woven cockade and a gray Luftwaffe eagle in embossed metal, the latter being secured with two hooks. The crown of the officers' cap is piped with dull silver-gray piping. The goggles are strapped on. The short sleeve shirt is made of sand colored cloth and has five buttons down the front. The pleated pockets have pointed flaps. The removable buttons are made of brown synthetic material (only the shoulder tab buttons are the dull gray and pebbled). The chest eagle is woven in light beige thread on a triangular tan backing.

Made of thick tan cloth, the tunic has an open collar and six buttons down the front. The collar is secured with a hook and eye. The chest pleated pockets and the bellow pockets on the skirt have straight edged buttoned flaps. All the buttons - including those on the shoulder straps - are the same size. Secured by split rings, they are finished in dark brown. Each cuff shows a false turn-up simulated by a row of stitches. An field dressing pocket is sewn inside the right hand side panel.

The cuff title is stitched 14 cm above the sleeve edge. The ribbon of the Iron Cross 2nd Class is threaded and stitched through the second button down the front, while the Iron Cross 1st Class and the pilot badge are pinned onto the left chest pocket, under the gilt clasp with device awarded for 200 missions. The Knight's Cross of the Iron Cross hangs from the neck with a smaller pattern ribbon.

The regulation chest eagle is woven in off-white thread on a beige backing. Both the officer's belt with pronged buckle and the ankle boots with eight eyelets are made of brown leather.

The tan trousers are gathered at the waist by a cloth strap and steel buckle. The slanted side pockets have no flaps, unlike the hip and thigh pockets. The loose fitting trousers legs are tapered and gathered around the ankles with a buckle and strap arrangement, reinforced with a button tab. All buttons are made of tan synthetic material, including those stitched inside at waist level for the braces.

49

'HINDENBURG' BOMBER PILOT

The captain's 'Schirmmütze' is cut in fine blue cloth. The eagle is embroidered in aluminum bullion. The band sports a hand-painted cockade and stylized wings, embroidered in aluminum bullion. The silver color chin strap is held by small silver buttons. The black vulcanized fiber peak has an oilcloth binding. The officer wears a civilian shirt with black tie.

The Knight's Cross hangs from its black, white and red ribbon. The tunic is made of the same cloth as the cap. It has four buttons down the front, and its four pleated pockets have straight edged flaps. All the pebbled buttons are silver color. The sleeves have turn-ups; the open collar is edged with an aluminum twisted piping. The shoulder tabs feature silver braid and two embossed rank stars, set on a bright yellow branch color underlay.

The yellow collar patches are piped in aluminum, with three woven wings over a half oak leaf wreath indicating the rank of captain. Woven in aluminum thread, the Luftwaffe eagle is stitched above the right chest pocket. The German Cross in Gold appears under the right chest pocket. The Luftwaffe heavy bomber gold clasp is pinned above the left chest pocket, above the Iron Cross 1st Class and the pilot badge. The 1941-42 Russian Campaign medal ribbon is stitched through the top buttonhole of the tunic. The unit cuff title is sewn on the left sleeve, one centimeter above the edge.

Gray suede gloves fastening with a pressure stud at the wrist.

The field gray blue trousers are slightly lighter than the tunic. The shoes are made black leather.

PILOT officer Helmut Sprung, a second lieutenant commissioned with the 7th Staffel of Kampfgeschwader 1, was awarded the Knight's Cross on 12 December 1943.

In the original picture below, Sprung is being congratulated by his comrades. When the photograph was taken at Neuburg, somewhere behind the Eastern Front on 5 August 1944, Sprung still sported the rank insignia of second lieutenant. Our reconstruction shows the officer a few months later after his promotion to the rank of captain.

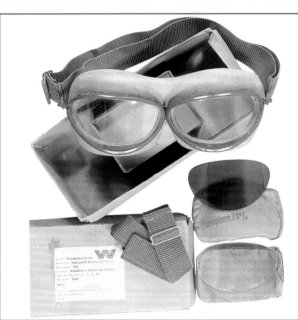

Above.
Manufactured by Philipp M. Winter on 1st September 1941, the flight goggle are shown in their original brown cardboard box. The goggles are fitted with a strong elasticated strap which can be adjusted by a sliding metal keeper. A spare strap is provided in the box, along with two pairs of plain and tinted lenses displayed here on their individual gray cloth pockets. The metal parts are painted green, the frame is made of thick, light brown rubber. To avoid damage, the lenses are kept in a partitioned case for transport.

The officer's flying helmet is made of fine brown leather, lined with lambskin. It accommodates earphones on each side. The chin strap is held by metal buckles. The goggles are attached to the helmet by two short tabs with snaps at the rear.

The airforce officer pattern belt is in light brown leather, with pebbled buckle and twin prongs.

The flying gloves are made of supple light brown leather, lined with rabbit fur. A tightening strap is located on the wrist.

The black flying boots are made of smooth leather for the uppers and suede for the shaft. A vertical zipper is set in on the inside of the shin; long buckled straps for tightening are located at the top and on the instep.

Above.
The flying suit is made of sturdy dark blue cloth, fully lined with the same synthetic fur as the wide collar. The suit has a sturdy zip down the front, running from the left thigh to the right shoulder. A large triangular yoke covers the right shoulder. A chest pocket with a vertical opening is set in near the neck. The two black leather tabs at the front are used to fasten the radio lead connecting to the back of the helmet. On the left hand side, a triangular cloth flap covers the ring used for quickly undonning the suit. The cuff zip fasteners are reinforced with pressure stud straps. Two vertical slits at hip level provide access to garments worn underneath. The fly, the leg bottoms and the leg horizontal and vertical pockets have zip fasteners, all manufactured by Elite, Rapid Zipp of Berlin. The zip tabs are made of brown leather. Connecting to the aircraft's heating system, the plugs at the cuffs, legs and under the vertical pockets are protected by gray leather tabs.

The officer pattern unit cuff title is made of dark blue wool. The 'Geschwader Hindenburg' inscription is done on aluminum thread. The title is shown as sewn on the sleeve, hence the missing letters at each end. Kampfgeschwader 1 took its name from Marshall Paul von Beneckendorff und von Hindenburg who defeated the Russians at Tannenberg in 1914.
Left.
The German Cross in Gold case is made of wood and black cardboard, lined with white sateen. The Iron Cross 1st Class case is similar but its bottom is lined with beige velvet and its lid with white sateen. The bomber Gold Clasp is presented in a dark blue case made of wood and cardboard. The bottom of the case is creamy white, and the inner face of the lid is made of light yellow sateen. The case for the pilot badge is made of the same materials as before but in very dark blue. The inner side of the lined in sateen and the bottom made of velvet. All four cases are fitted with a spring-loaded lock.

'REICHSFÜHRER' SS GRENADIER

Formed around a cadre of 28th RFSS (Reichsführer SS) Sturmbrigade elements, the 16th SS Pz. Gren. Div. 'Reichsführer SS' was raised in October 1943.

Posted to Corsica, it soon became the only force capable of successfully opposing the increasing activities of the local partisans. When French troops landed in Corsica in 1944, the 16th RFSS withdrew to the Bastia-Bonifacio area prior to being shipped to Italy. The move was conducted with light losses. In January 1944, elements of 35th SS Pz. Gren. Rgt. (one of the division's two grenadier regiments), fought Allied troops in the Nettuno-Anzio beachhead. Transferred to Hungary for refitting in April 1944, the division was ferried back to Italy in May where it distinguished itself by checking the British 8th Army between Parma and Grossetto. From August to September, the division fought its way up Italy during the German withdrawal and, during the retreat, severely clashed with Italian partisans in the south of Bologna.

Note: the uniforms shown here were those worn by the 16th RFSS in Corsica and Italy.

The SS-Panzergrenadier (private) wears a light tan cotton shirt. The garment has four buttons down the front, buttoned cuffs, and a yoke covering the torso down to the chest pleated box-pockets. The shoulder tabs are piped in white (service color of the division's 'Panzergrenadiers'). The Waffen-SS pattern eagle is sewn on the left sleeve. Made of synthetic material, the front and collar buttons are the same color as the shirt, with only those on the shoulder tabs being made of brown finished metal. The shorts are kept up by a black leather belt fitted with an aluminum buckle. Their metal hooks at the waist double as belt keepers.

Right.
Close-up of the tropical shirt and its insignia. For improved camouflage, the steel helmet has received a coat of sand yellow paint over its original field gray finish.

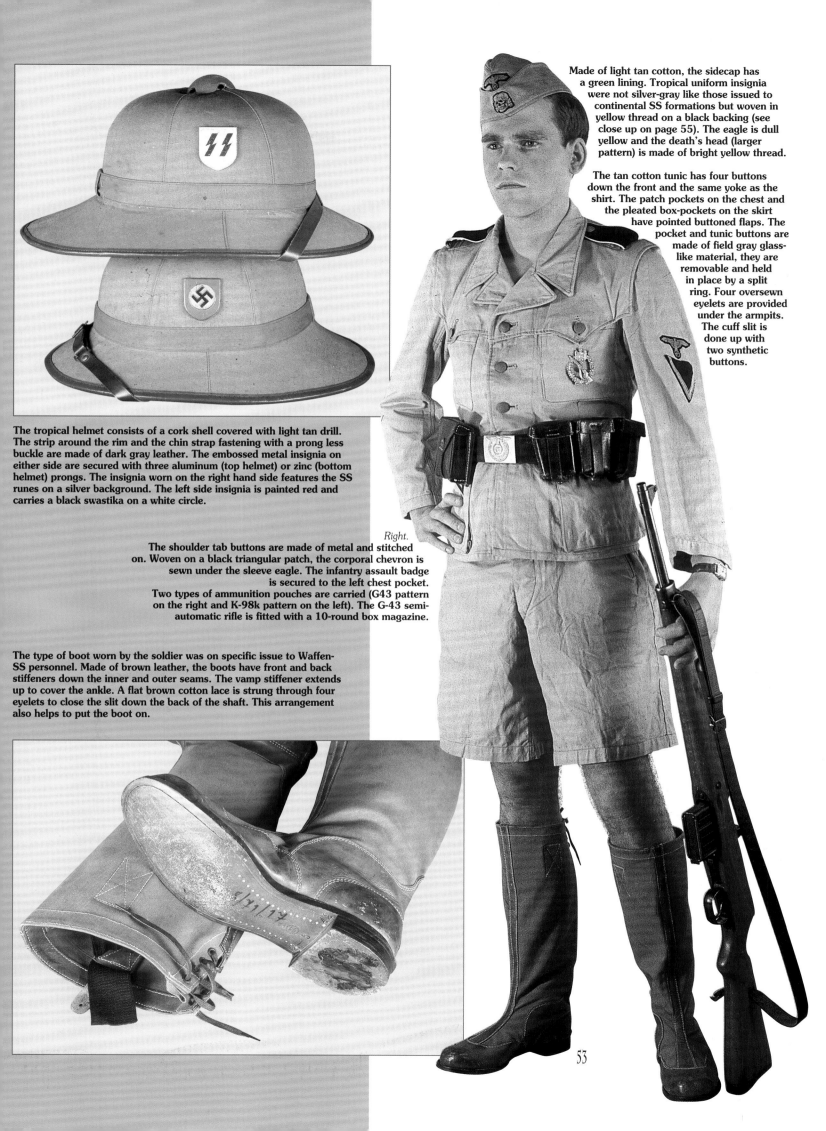

Made of light tan cotton, the sidecap has a green lining. Tropical uniform insignia were not silver-gray like those issued to continental SS formations but woven in yellow thread on a black backing (see close up on page 55). The eagle is dull yellow and the death's head (larger pattern) is made of bright yellow thread.

The tan cotton tunic has four buttons down the front and the same yoke as the shirt. The patch pockets on the chest and the pleated box-pockets on the skirt have pointed buttoned flaps. The pocket and tunic buttons are made of field gray glass-like material, they are removable and held in place by a split ring. Four oversewn eyelets are provided under the armpits. The cuff slit is done up with two synthetic buttons.

The tropical helmet consists of a cork shell covered with light tan drill. The strip around the rim and the chin strap fastening with a prong less buckle are made of dark gray leather. The embossed metal insignia on either side are secured with three aluminum (top helmet) or zinc (bottom helmet) prongs. The insignia worn on the right hand side features the SS runes on a silver background. The left side insignia is painted red and carries a black swastika on a white circle.

Right.

The shoulder tab buttons are made of metal and stitched on. Woven on a black triangular patch, the corporal chevron is sewn under the sleeve eagle. The infantry assault badge is secured to the left chest pocket. Two types of ammunition pouches are carried (G43 pattern on the right and K-98k pattern on the left). The G-43 semi-automatic rifle is fitted with a 10-round box magazine.

The type of boot worn by the soldier was on specific issue to Waffen-SS personnel. Made of brown leather, the boots have front and back stiffeners down the inner and outer seams. The vamp stiffener extends up to cover the ankle. A flat brown cotton lace is strung through four eyelets to close the slit down the back of the shaft. This arrangement also helps to put the boot on.

53

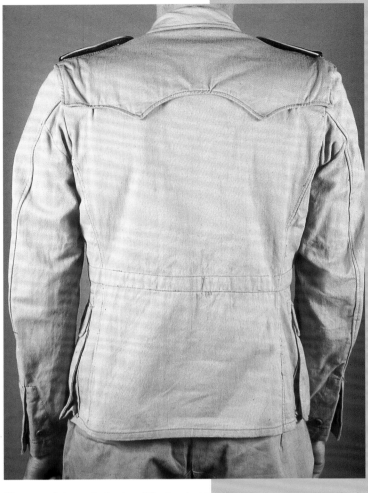

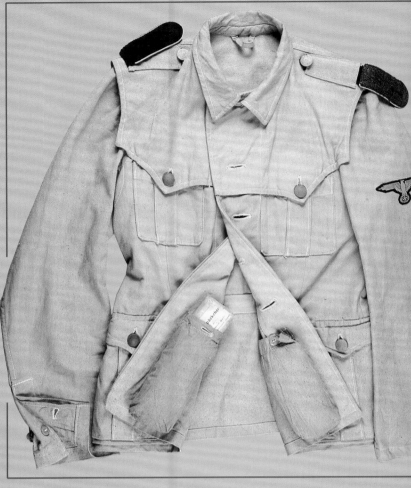

Close-up of the typical yoke of the tropical tunic covering the top of the back and extending down the front into two pointed flap pockets.
Of note are the cuff slits and the seams of the drawstring at waist level.

Early type of tunic (pleated box pockets) made of sturdy cotton twill. The two field dressing pockets in the inner front panels are clearly shown. Late type tunics have a different shoulder tab securing arrangement and are devoid of collar buttons.

The 'Reichsführer SS' cuff title (not worn on any of the tropical uniforms illustrated in this article).

The shorts worn by the grenadier are cut in light cotton cloth. The slanted slide pockets have buttons. The fly has five buttons. The fob watch has a horizontal opening. The six flat hooks at waist level are painted and stitched with the bent part down. The shorts are adjusted with a buckle strap on each hip. The braces are fastened with two buttons at the front and two button tabs at the back. The lining (shorts and pockets) is made of white cloth. All buttons are made of dark brown synthetic material.

Another type of shorts cut in the same cloth as the previous garment. The pointed flaps of the fob and hip pockets have yellow-orange synthetic buttons. The others are made of wood.

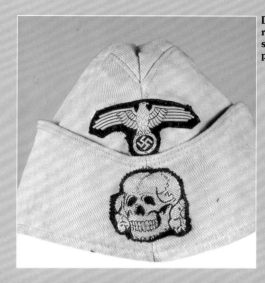

Detail of the other ranks' pattern sidecap (see also page 53)

Right, and above, left.
Cut in light tan cotton, the cap of this 'Rottenführer' (corporal) is unlined and sports two insignia on the front. Both are woven, the eagle in bright yellow thread, and the death's head in dull yellow. Our man has a tunic similar to the figure on page 53, all buttons are made of glass like yellowish-green material. Sleeve badges are show below: the eagle is embroidered in dull flat yellow thread, the corporal stripes are in bright yellow on a black overlay.

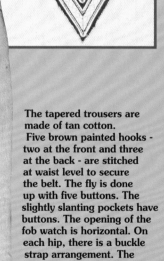

The tapered trousers are made of tan cotton.
Five brown painted hooks - two at the front and three at the back - are stitched at waist level to secure the belt. The fly is done up with five buttons. The slightly slanting pockets have buttons. The opening of the fob watch is horizontal. On each hip, there is a buckle strap arrangement. The braces connect to buttons at the front and tabs at the back. The lining is in white cloth. The seat of the trousers is reinforced from the groin up. The tapered legs are gathered around the ankles with a thin strap and two cloth strips. The two hip pockets button in the same way as the front ones. The buttons are made of brown and sand synthetic material.

ENGINEER, EASTERN FRONT

Made of field gray cloth, the 1935 Pattern tunic shows extensive wear. The dark bluish-green serge collar is adorned with the regulation patches. The shoulder tabs, in the same material, are piped in black for the engineers. The battalion number is embroidered in black and outlined in white. The box pleated pockets have three-pointed flaps. The chest eagle is woven in gray thread on a light field gray backing. The corporal chevron on a dark green background is worn on the left sleeve.

The winter cotton trousers (1943 Pattern) are padded with wool and gathered by a drawstring around the ankles. The splinter camouflage pattern consists of soft-edged blotches of medium green and brown on a light field gray backing. The loose fitting trousers can be worn over the regulation field gray trousers.

The sapper also carries two stick grenades and a 'Teller' anti-tank mine

Soviet shelling intensified into a pounding, ominously forewarning that a Russian attack was in the offing.

Outnumbered, the German soldiers of the 34th Infantry Division manning the front line evacuated their position at dusk. Only groups of the 34th Engineer Battalion were left behind to turn into a 'Teufelsgarten' (devil's playground) the trenches, the strongholds and the front line positions abandoned by their comrades. Soon, the engineers had completed their deadly task: the few remaining buildings, the ford and the sunken track leading to the command post had also been turned into lethal traps.

Making the most of their redoubtable skills, the German sappers had again managed to check the Soviets by channeling their forces into a 'mine blockade.'

The engineer corporal's load consists mostly of explosive blocks in the two side pouches and back pack of his 'Pioniersturmgepäck' (engineer assault pack). For easier reach, the gas mask is carried in the rubber-lined outer pocket of the right hand pouch. The two web straps securing the pouch flap are reinforced with a string tie. The main compartment of the side pouch holds a three-kilogram charge. Both pouches also have four snap-fastening rifle clip pockets on the front edges. The flap of each compartment has a metal reinforced strap fitting into a steel buckle.

The three components of the engineer's assault pack - the backpack and the two side pouches - are cut in sturdy olive green canvas. The left hand pouch is subdivided into two compartments - each carrying a one-kilogramme explosive charge - and four rifle clip pockets (as the right hand one). The side pouches are secured to the belt with loops are held together with an adjustable web strap in the back. A saw carried in black leather sheath and a bayonet are fastened to the belt.

The backpack is fastened to the black leather suspension straps. It has four compartments. For easier reach, the explosive blocks are stacked in the side-opening compartment on the right-hand side. The 'Zeltbahn' (tent section) has been folded in the back compartment for padding. The mess kit is carried in the upper compartment where it is secured with two tie strings.

Right.
The bread bag and water bottle are carried on the hip in the usual way.

Right.
Yellow triangular flags are used to mark safe lanes through minefields. The carrier is made of black artificial leather and contains about a dozen flags. It has an adjustable webbing sling, and two belt loops. The large oblong flag is a mine marker.
The short steel and bakelite wirecutters are carried in a black artificial leather cover with leather reinforced flap. The cover is attached to the belt by means of two leather loops.

57

PARATROOPER, THE UKRAINE

The reversible quilted trousers are kept up with braces stitched at the back and buttons at the front. The triangular fly has eight buttons. The standard side pockets have button flaps. The legs secure with a white ankle drawstring. All the buttons are made of blue-gray finished metal.

From Norway to Denmark and from Holland to Belgium, German paratroopers were at the vanguard of Hitler's forces during the opening moves of the Blitzkrieg.

After seizing key points and airfields, the airborne soldiers won fame for capturing fortresses which stood in the way of the panzers. In Greece, the German paras captured the Corinth Canal and later, stormed the island of Crete at a terrible cost. By 1943, some para units were deployed on the Smolensk front in the Ukraine.

The Luftwaffe airborne qualification badge was awarded after six jumps. The badge shown here is well crafted and consists of a copper-nickel alloy wreath (oak leaf pattern on the left and laurel on the right) onto which a diving brass eagle is secured. The eagle clutches a swastika in its talons.

The turn-up of the field gray 'Feldmütze' is fastened with two buttons (smaller pattern, finished in field gray). The embroidered national cockade is sewn below the eagle, embroidered in gray on a field blue underlay. The blue gray 'Fliegerbluse' has a fly front covering six black synthetic buttons. The removable shoulder tabs are made of blue-gray cloth. Piped in yellow (the service color of paratroopers), they are secured near the collar by two small gilt buttons. The yellow collar tabs bear the single metal wing of private rank. Embroidered in gray thread, the eagle insignia appears on the right side of the chest. The airborne qualification badge is pinned on the left side.

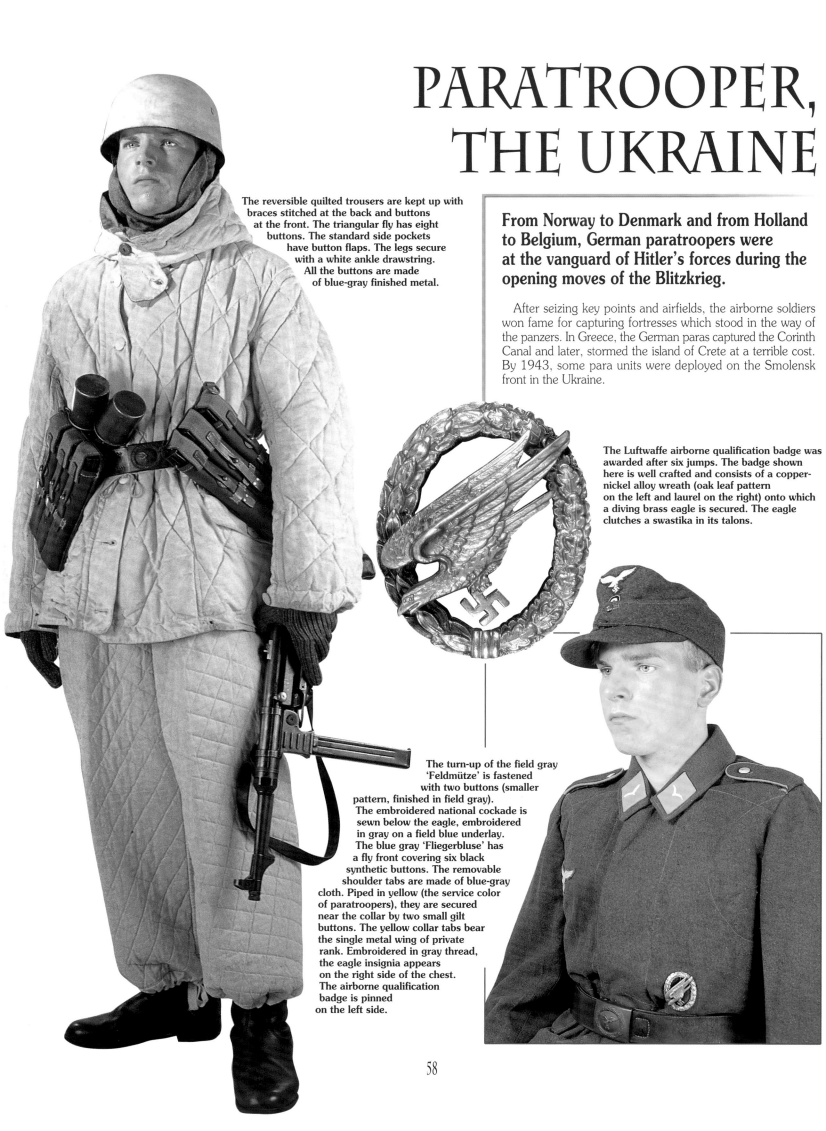

Cut from thick cotton material, the green parka is reversible in white. The parka is darker than the trousers, which look more grayish. Intended for wear in the cold season, both garments are double quilted with wool off-cuts to form a lozenge pattern on the parka and small squares on the trousers.

Daubed in white to match the landscape, the paratrooper's helmet is worn over a stretchable balaklava helmet knitted in gray wool. The helmet is held with two 'Y' straps connecting at the back but skirting the ears. To fasten the helmet, the lower portion of the right chin strap was slipped through a quick release buckle and then secured onto an adjustable side loop.

The shell of the helmet is made of thick sheet steel (1.15 mm thick carbon, manganese and chromium alloy with 220kg/sq. mm tempering strength). The helmet liner is made of two plain kid leather pieces (pig's hide is also known to have been used) with 12 ventilation holes. The liner has an aluminum (or alloy) ring which is secured to the helmet with four bolts doubling as vent holes. Between the metal ring and the leather lining, seven foam rubber pads are fitted to act as shock absorbers. The two 'Y' straps can be adjusted to fit the back of the wearer's head by three sets of spanner bolts. The chin strap components are made of gray kid leather lined with chamois skin.

Fitted with a blue-gray finished Luftwaffe buckle, the black leather belt holds two stick grenades and canvas and leather magazine pouches for the submachine-gun.

The parka has a thick padded hood which protects against the cold and provides camouflage effect when worn with the green side out. Like the trousers, it is lined with wool off-cuts and reinforced with square pattern quilting. A tab with two buttons covers the throat when the garment is worn with either green or white side out. On either side of the hood, there is a large metal eyelet for a drawstring (missing here).

59

LUFTWAFFE ASSAULT GUN CREW

The drill smock (worn over the 'Fliegerbluse') is not reversible. The camouflage pattern consists of sharp edged brown and medium green blotches loosely printed over a field gray background.

The pattern is completed by vertical thin green stripes. The five buttons down the front are made of dark blue synthetic material. The collar is fitted with a metal hook. Two small vents are provided under the armpits. The cuffs are gathered with a strap and black dished metal buttons. Wide and deep, the hip pockets close with a buttoned flap.

Woven in white thread on a blue-gray backing, the Luftwaffe eagle appears on the right side of the chest. The shoulder tabs of the warrant officer are made of field gray cloth. They are piped in scarlet (the service color of assault gun units) and secured at the shoulder seam with an loop in uniform cloth. The silver braid and the two embossed metal stars on the tabs were for senior NCOs. The embossed metal 'death's heads' (identical to the Army armored force insignia) are pinned directly onto the lapels.

Right.
The steel helmet is finished in gray. The off-white Luftwaffe eagle appears on its left side. Secured by a pronged buckle, the chin strap is black on its outer side. The round neck gray wool jersey is a privately purchased garment.

Eastern Front, late 1943 early 1944. The outposts held by the 5th Luftwaffe Field Division are being subjected to a short but intense shelling by Russian artillery. Harried by the spirited enemy, the dazed survivors fall back.

The barrels of the MG-42s glow red as the machine-gunners loose off burst after burst into the Russian waves. Under their withering crossfire, the Russian assault is beaten back but then numerous T-34s enter the fray and threaten to break through to the German battalion's main defenses.

The 'Sturmgeschütze' led by Lieutenant Wolfgang Bach are then called in to plug the gap.

The chest eagle and the shoulder straps are identical to those used on the camouflage smock. The Luftwaffe NCO braid is sewn around the edge of the collar. The lapels are adorned with the same metal 'death's heads' as worn on the camouflage smock in compliance with the dress regulations issued to the crews of the 3rd Assault Gun Battery 'Sturmgeschütze' of the 5th Self-Propelled Anti-Tank Gun unit (Panzerjägerabteilung 5). The Iron Cross 1st Class
and the Ground Combat Badge are pinned on the chest. The 'Kuban' shield is secured to the left sleeve.

Designed by Prof. Von Weech of Berlin,
the Lufwaffe Ground Combat Badge was
instituted by Göring
on 31 March 1942.
The award consists
of a wreath of oak leaves,
a Luftwaffe eagle
and a cloud from which
a lightning bolt strikes
the ground. The insignia
is cast in zinc alloy while
the embossed metal
eagle is finished in dull
silver and secured with
a rivet. The gray paint
covering the insignia
has practically worn off.
The badge was awarded
to soldiers who has
been involved in three
engagements on three
different days.

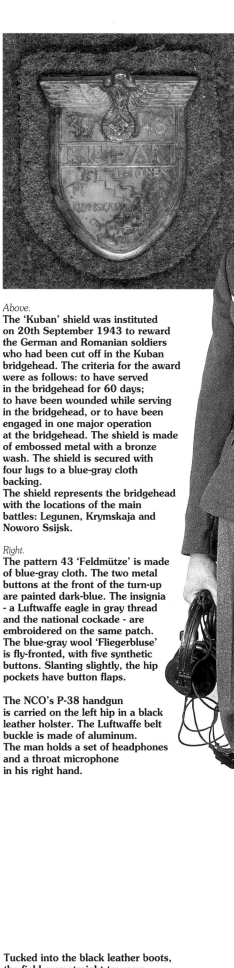

Above.
The 'Kuban' shield was instituted on 20th September 1943 to reward the German and Romanian soldiers who had been cut off in the Kuban bridgehead. The criteria for the award were as follows: to have served in the bridgehead for 60 days; to have been wounded while serving in the bridgehead, or to have been engaged in one major operation at the bridgehead. The shield is made of embossed metal with a bronze wash. The shield is secured with four lugs to a blue-gray cloth backing.
The shield represents the bridgehead with the locations of the main battles: Legunen, Krymskaja and Noworo Ssijsk.

Right.
The pattern 43 'Feldmütze' is made of blue-gray cloth. The two metal buttons at the front of the turn-up are painted dark-blue. The insignia - a Luftwaffe eagle in gray thread and the national cockade - are embroidered on the same patch. The blue-gray wool 'Fliegerbluse' is fly-fronted, with five synthetic buttons. Slanting slightly, the hip pockets have button flaps.

The NCO's P-38 handgun is carried on the left hip in a black leather holster. The Luftwaffe belt buckle is made of aluminum. The man holds a set of headphones and a throat microphone in his right hand.

Tucked into the black leather boots, the field gray straight trousers are regulation issue.

HEER INFANTRYMAN, EASTERN FRONT

Pattern 1943 parka worn with camouflage side out. The pattern is inspired by the pattern 1931 'Zeltbahn' (tent section). The three-tone camouflage scheme consists of broken lines with sharp edges. The suit is made of cotton and lined with wool off-cuts.

The rifle ammo pouches are fastened to the black leather belt. The soldier has secured a stick grenade and his helmet to his belt. The camouflage helmet cover is fastened with a drawstring around the rim.

Pattern 1942 field gray cap with rabbit fur lining.

The wear and tear on the helmet cover dates this reconstruction to winter 1943-44. Like the helmet cover, the reversible padded parka and trousers set were introduced in autumn 1943. This uniform was only issued to Heer field infantry units on combat duties.

For better hearing, the hood has round ear openings, showing the gray wool padding material. The manufacturer's trademark, 'E. Reitz Antwerpen,' is stamped in ink inside the right flap.

The padded mittens are lined with rabbit fur. They are tightened at the wrist with tapes. This model was also available with wool padding.

1943 Pattern reversible winter trousers. These are made of the same material as the parka but display a marked difference in colors. The bottom of the legs secure over the boots with cloth tapes.

Thanks to this removable device (winter trigger), soldiers could fire their rifles with their winter mittens on. In addition to the separate thumb, some mittens had an unlined index finger so the soldier could pull the trigger more easily.

The 1943 camouflage suit was worn with the white side out to better merge with snowy surroundings. The buttons sewn on the upper sleeves (on both sides) are used to secure colored identification strips.

K-98k rifle.

The reversible parka has 10 buttons down the front and an overlapping front closure. The garment is fastened with a cloth belt, and a drawstring at the bottom. The unlined hood secures with tapes; the cuffs are gathered with cloth straps and buttons.

The trousers have overlapping buttoned flaps on the fly. Like those on the pocket flaps, the five buttons - only one is showing here - are made of ceramic or painted metal. The trousers are kept up with removable cotton braces.

Below.
Pattern 1942 felt boots made of high grade leather (two of the numerous variants on regular issue). Of note are the toe caps and the various securing arrangements at the top of the shafts (missing from some versions).

Eentrenching tool, bayonet, bread bag, mess tin and water bottle.

63

1944

RADIO OPERATOR

The shirt is made of fine green cotton. It ¾ closes all the way to the waist with four green cardboard buttons. The box pleated pockets have three-pointed flaps with metal buttons finished in field gray. Like those on the tunic, the buttons are removable thanks to split rings. The private's shoulder tabs are piped in lemon yellow (the service color of army signals). Woven in light gray thread on a triangular pale green background, the eagle is stitched above the right chest pocket. Embroidered on a pale green backing, the mountain rifle's edelweiss insignia is worn on the right sleeve.

In 1944, on the Italian Front, the Allies stepped up their offensive and rapidly skirted the German lines held by the 14th Panzer Corps to the south and the 51st Mountain Corps farther north.

The two 'Funker' (radio operators) depicted in this study are seen somewhere between Arce and Ceprano. They belong to a small intelligence group transmitting data to the 51st Mountain Corps from their hideout set up on a rocky outcrop. Soon, the German artillery will open fire on the Allies, smashing bridges and pounding assembly areas before a possible counter-attack.

The operator carries a telephone cable reel on his chest. Manufactured in 1939 by Expresswerke AG, the reel is fitted with a thick carrying strap adjusting around the carrier's waist. For improved comfort, the metal frames have thick leather-reinforced canvas padding.

The brown leather pouch fitted to the waist cushion holds various tools. The tubular frame is finished in green. Thus equipped, the transmitter can quickly pay out the line by operating the crank. The telephone line is about 300 m long.

When carried on the radio operator's back, the leather strap which works the braking device on the cable reel is clearly visible

Above.

The 1943 Pattern 'Feldmütze' is made of green canvas (the same material as used for the mountain rifles' 'Feldjacke'). The turn-up is kept up with two silver buttons. Unlined but fitted with an inner leather band, the cap has a long peak and no ventilation grommets. The insignia are combined on a T-shaped backing. The eagle is woven in gray thread on a pale green underlay. The sleeve edelweiss and the chest eagle are woven in the same material. Invisible when viewed from this side, an embossed metal edelweiss is pinned to the left side of the cap. Slipped through five loops on the shorts (two on the front and three on the back), the black leather belt is fitted with a steel buckle finished in field gray.

Below.

The shorts are made of 'reed green' drill. The fly has six buttons of yellowish synthetic material. The waist adjusts with a strap and pronged buckle arrangement. The slanted hip pockets have no buttons. The fob watch has a steel ring for securing a chain. The pocket on the right hip has one button. The lining, pockets and crotch reinforcement are made of white cotton.

This other model of telephone wire reel is finished in green and has the same carrying capacity as the one used by the man on the right. The simplified pattern reel is fitted with brown leather straps.

The second operator wears a 1943 Pattern field cap, cut in green canvas with stitched-on fake turn-up. Like the cockade, the eagle is woven in dull gray thread on a pale green backing. The crown is lined with green cloth and reinforced with a leather band. Both trousers and cap are issue items whereas the smock has been locally-made in camouflage cloth. The splinter camouflage pattern consists of green and brown broken lines over a light field gray background. The garment is done up with five buttons down the front. The patch pockets have three-pointed flaps; the cuffs secure with a metal button. All the other buttons are made of green synthetic material.

The trousers have 14 dished metal buttons (smaller pattern and finished in field gray): eight around the waist for the braces, five for the fly and one at the hip pocket. The legs are straight. The vertical side pockets and the fob pocket have no buttons. The half-belt on the small of the back adjusts with a black painted metal buckle. The lining is made of green sateen and the pockets are cut in white cotton.

Next to a hand-held wire reel is an M-33 field telephone 'Feldfernsprecher 33' carried in its brown bakelite case. The metal fittings and the receiver are finished in black. This model was manufactured in 1943. When the box lid is closed, the receiver is held down with a spring clip.

The radio set 'Feldfernsprecher B' is secured to the heavy black leather harness. The set is fitted with its headset and throat microphone. The aerial is unfolded for transmitting and receiving. The P-08 holster is secured to the black belt fitted with a field gray buckle.

The mountain boots are made of reddish-brown leather over which stiff field gray canvas anklets are ¾ worn.

PARATROOPER, CASSINO

The helmet is covered with regulation camouflage netting as often seen during the Cassino battle. The trousers' two front and two back slit pockets have button flaps like the thigh patch pocket. The tapered trousers legs have the same fastening arrangement as the belt.

Armament includes a stick grenade and an MP-40 submachine-gun. The magazines for the SMG are carried in pouches at the belt. Leather equipment (such as ammunition pouches and the P-08 holster) issued to Luftwaffe personnel was brown in color.

On the Italian front, the Mount Cassino monastery — a celebrated shrine of Christianity — was turned to rubble by Allied bombers on 15 February 1944.

The ruins were quickly occupied by the paratroopers of the Luftwaffe 1st Fallschirmjäger Division. The German paras deployed in the Italian theater were clad in a mixture of standard airborne equipment and clothing issued during the North African campaign.

Above.
The pullover summer shirt has long sleeves. The front opening, down to the waist, is done up with four buttons; the box pleated chest pockets have a flap and painted button. The Luftwaffe insignia include an eagle embroidered in gray cotton on a triangular underlay plus regulation shoulder tabs piped in yellow and adorned with the two silver stars of a 'Stabsfeldwebel' with 12 years' service. Made of cotton, the 1941 Pattern trousers are fastened at the waist with a hemmed-in belt fitted with a pronged buckle of light metal. The 1938 Pattern paratrooper helmet is painted sand for camouflage.

Opposite page.
The jump trousers are kept up with braces. The front pocket flaps close with pressure studs and the hip pockets with buttons. The vertical pocket for the gravity knife on the right thigh has a triangular flap with two studs. The field dressing was carried in a vertical fob pocket on the left leg and sealing with three pressure studs. Secured to the shell by an aluminum ring, the helmet liner has 12 ventilation holes and rubber pads. The chin straps are made of gray leather secured to the shell with four bolts (one on either side and two at the back), and adjustable with two snaps.

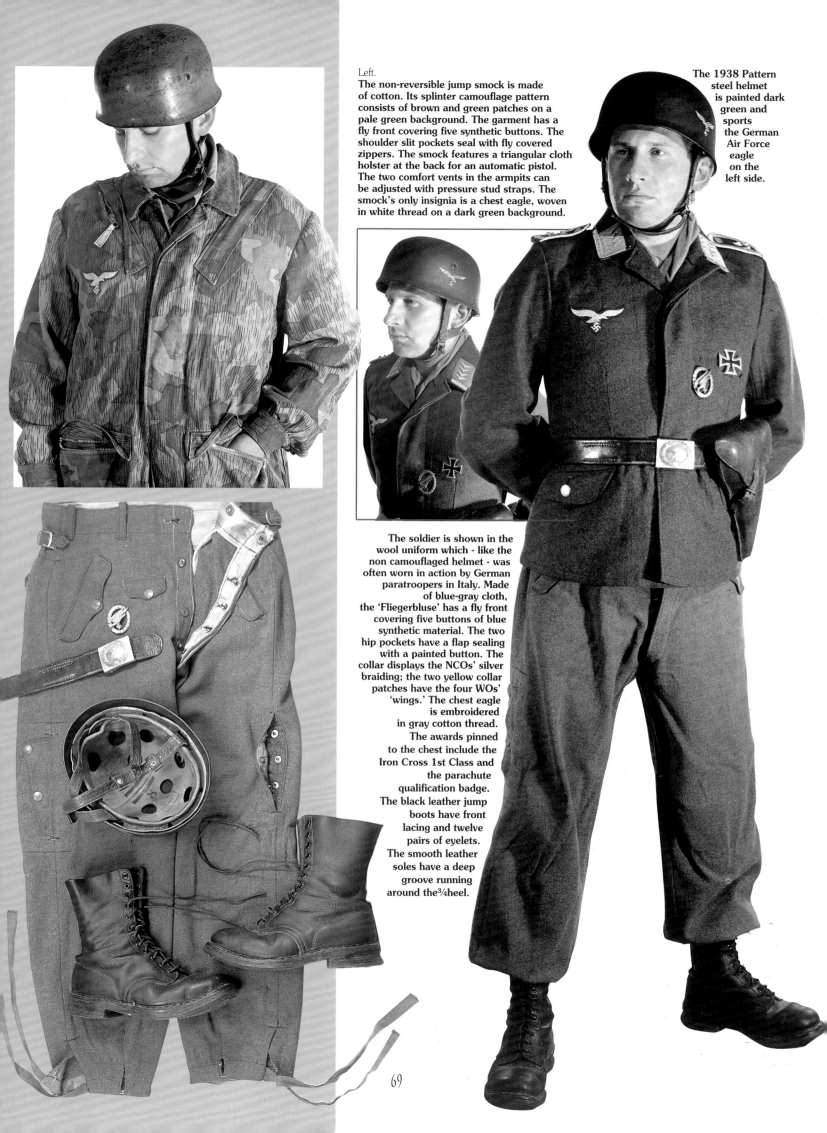

Left.

The non-reversible jump smock is made of cotton. Its splinter camouflage pattern consists of brown and green patches on a pale green background. The garment has a fly front covering five synthetic buttons. The shoulder slit pockets seal with fly covered zippers. The smock features a triangular cloth holster at the back for an automatic pistol. The two comfort vents in the armpits can be adjusted with pressure stud straps. The smock's only insignia is a chest eagle, woven in white thread on a dark green background.

The 1938 Pattern steel helmet is painted dark green and sports the German Air Force eagle on the left side.

The soldier is shown in the wool uniform which - like the non camouflaged helmet - was often worn in action by German paratroopers in Italy. Made of blue-gray cloth, the 'Fliegerbluse' has a fly front covering five buttons of blue synthetic material. The two hip pockets have a flap sealing with a painted button. The collar displays the NCOs' silver braiding; the two yellow collar patches have the four WOs' 'wings.' The chest eagle is embroidered in gray cotton thread. The awards pinned to the chest include the Iron Cross 1st Class and the parachute qualification badge. The black leather jump boots have front lacing and twelve pairs of eyelets. The smooth leather soles have a deep groove running around the ¾ heel.

THE 1944 PATTERN ARMY UNIFORM

The peak of the 1943 pattern field cap is stitched around the edge for stiffening. The suspension straps, belt and rifle ammo pouches are made of black leather. The belt buckle is finished in dull aluminum. The gasmask carrier strap is slung over the left shoulder. The anklets are made of olive green canvas. The plain leather ankle boots have nine pairs of eyelets.

In spring 1943, German Army High Command issued requirements for the development of a new uniform.

The uniform was ready in summer and soon issued for testing to the following units: the 17th and 73rd Infantry Divisions; the 78th 'Sturmdivision' (assault infantry division), the 28th and 104th 'Jägerdivisions' (light infantry), the 2nd Mountain Rifle Division, the 16th Panzer Division and the 'Ersatzbrigade Großdeutschland' (mechanised infantry).

The officers of these units were briefed with reporting to High Command about the modifications and improvements they felt the uniform needed. The new pattern was officially approved on 8 July 1944 with delivery starting seven weeks later. Although official directives specified that the color of the uniform was to be 'olive brown,' this was not strictly enforced as field gray (or even gray) cloth is also known to have been used.

The uniform used for this study fully complies with regulations but variations have been noticed: some other ranks' jackets have cuff turn-ups like the officer's while others have box pleated pockets with three-pointed flaps. Also, the legs of some trousers secure with ankle lacing while others don't.

The jacket and trousers are cut in 'olive brown' reworked wool cloth. The jacket has a fly front covering six gray finished buttons, two of which are stitched on the waistband. The collar can be kept up thanks to a tab stitched under the collar at left and a button at the right (an optional arrangement). The flaps on the chest patch pockets have straight edges. Running down from the elbow, the sleeve slits (visible on the opposite page) secure with a button fitting into one of two horizontal buttonholes. The lining is made of fine gray cotton like the two inner pockets fitted with a pressed cardboard button. The chest eagle is not woven but printed on a triangular backing (late directive not strictly enforced) in dark green, green and gray. The collar tabs ('Litzen') are woven in gray thread. The late-war, olive-brown wool shoulder straps have grass green piping for the Panzergrenadiers. The tabs are secured by a loop at the arm seam and a button near the collar.

Above.
Displayed on a 1944 Pattern bread bag are the weapon cleaning kit, a yellow plastic edible fat box and a new pattern bayonet in its scabbard.

The 1944 Pattern straight trousers are cut in thick 'olive brown' cloth. They can be kept up either with braces or with the regulation belt slipped through eight loops (see overleaf). The fly has four buttons, a fifth one is provided under the front, behind the belt. The slanted side pockets seal with button flaps. The button flaps for the fob and hip pockets have straight edges. The trousers lining and the pockets are made of whitish cotton. The trousers' 'dished type' metal buttons are painted gray. The two trouser belts (late type) are made of thick olive green webbing. The top belt securing device (replacing the regulation buckle) has a black leather reinforcement. Painted gray, its pronged buckle is the same as that used for the assault pack. Leather is also used on the second belt to strengthen the tips and to provide a thin strip for the buckle eyelets.

The man's 1942 Pattern steel helmet is painted field gray. Secured to the leather suspension straps with hooks, the assault pack consists of a trapezoid semi-rigid web frame. It supports the mess tin and a tubular pouch (see overleaf) here partly hidden by the camouflage tent section. The bread bag, to which the water bottle is hooked, is fastened to the belt. The gasmask carrier is placed next to the water bottle. The antigas cape in its green pouch is wrapped around the gasmask carrier. The entrenching tool in its black leather carrier is secured to the left side (concealing the frog of the new pattern bayonet secured to the belt). Metal pegs and coiled cord protrude from the rolled tent section.

THE 1944 PATTERN ARMY UNIFORM

Cut in green cotton material, the soldier's shirt has four black synthetic buttons down the front. The straight edged pocket flaps and the cuff straps use the same buttons. The loose fitting shirt reaches down to the thighs.

There are thin loops near the shoulder seam for the shoulder tabs. The private's ID tag and a religious medal hang from a black cord.

Trouser braces, made of thin gray material with metal buckles and cloth covered springs.

Trouser belts, made of thick gray webbing with metal and leather fittings.

The new pattern knife/bayonet measures 29.5 cm. The metal components are made of steel and the grips of bakelite. The pointed blade has a single sharp edge. The removable multipurpose tool fitting within the handle combines a bodkin (with a needle eye), a corkscrew, a tin opener, and screwdriver with a notch to strip rubber-coated wire. The steel scabbard is painted black.

Right.
The assault pack is made up with a webbing and metal frame that hooks onto the standard suspension straps. The frame supports an assortment of gear, including a tubular ditty bag (bottom), the mess kit, rolled tent section, etc. The frame metal parts are painted gray, the webbing shows several color variations.

OFFICER ON DUTY AT THE FÜHRER'S HQ

Wounded several times while leading his battalion in the field, this major has now been appointed to the Führer's HQ at Rastenburg in eastern Prussia.

On 9 April 1944, during a mission at Posen, the officer decided to relax by going to a show.

Thus attired, the officer is heading for a theater show. Cut in fine field gray woolen cloth, the crown of his 'Schirmmütze' (peaked cap) has the typical 'Sattelform' (saddle shaped) raised front of officers' caps. The piping of the dark bluish-green cap band is white (infantry). The aluminum cords are secured with silver finished buttons. The peak is made of black vulcanized fiber. The silver insignia are in embossed metal.

The double-breasted field gray greatcoat is cut from high-quality wool material, lined with green sateen. It has a double row of six pebbled metal buttons down the front. The slanted side pockets have broad flaps.

The cuff turn-ups are cut in matching cloth.

The shoulder tabs consist of flat aluminum braiding interwoven on a white underlay. The cuff title is sewn above the turn up on the left sleeve.

Dangling from two hangers secured to inner snap hooks, the Army officers' dress dagger is carried almost horizontally.

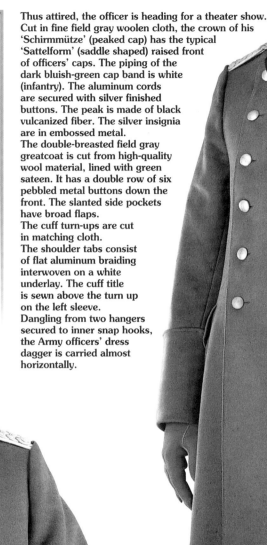

'Posdam' Pattern short black leather boots.

Left.
This Army dress dagger was crafted by Carl Eickhorn of Solingen. The metal parts are finished in dull silver. The handle is made of orange synthetic material. The guard eagle is almost identical to that worn on the cap. The scabbard is made of steel, and the hangers of dark green velvet enhanced with thin aluminum braiding. The metal components are coated in dull silver and decorated with an oak leaf motif. The gray suede gloves are made of pig's hide and secure with a pressure stud at the wrist. The theater ticket has been delivered by the Reichsgautheatre at Posen for a show scheduled for 9 September 1944. Cast in metal, the Gold Wound Badge was awarded to soldiers who had been wounded five times (or more) in action or been inflicted with one wound resulting in permanent disability.

The Iron cross 2d Class.

The piped tunic's collar is secured with two metal hooks. The white celluloid undercollar is fastened with three folding hooks. The tailor's cloth label, Carl Meyers of Köln, is sewn on the green sateen lining.

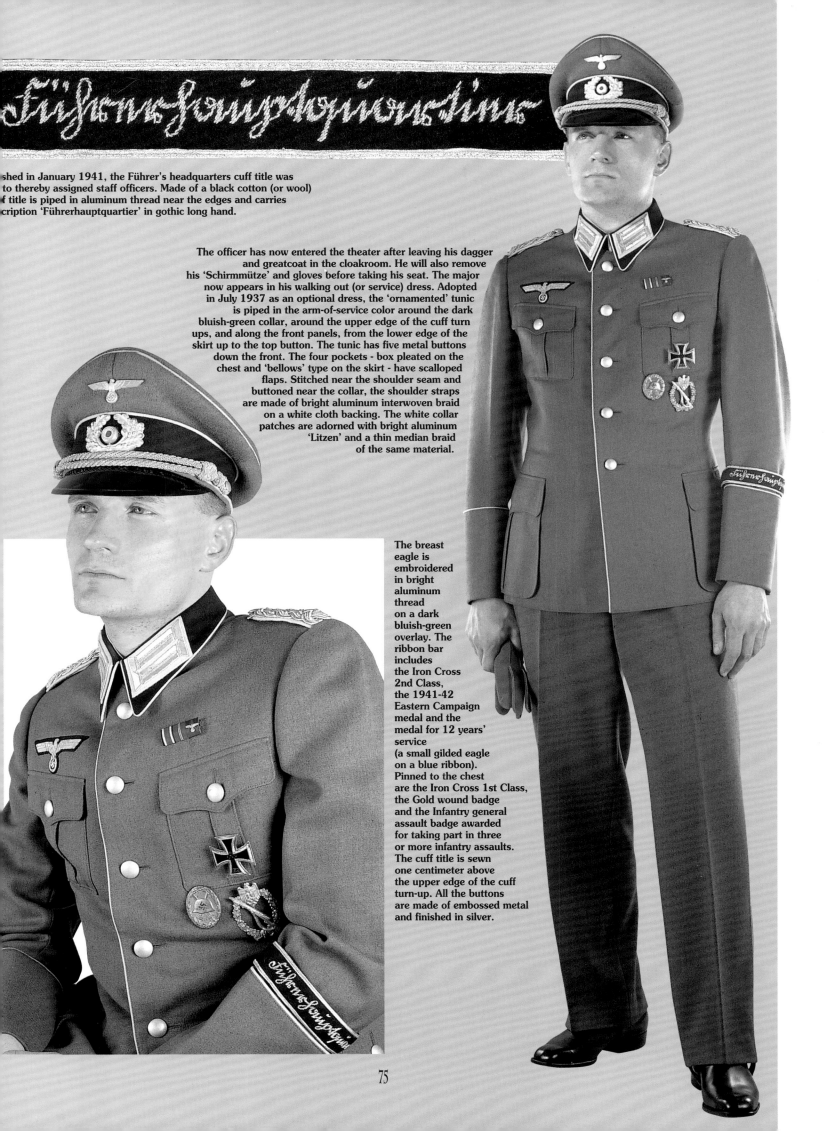

shed in January 1941, the Führer's headquarters cuff title was
to thereby assigned staff officers. Made of a black cotton (or wool)
title is piped in aluminum thread near the edges and carries
cription 'Führerhauptquartier' in gothic long hand.

The officer has now entered the theater after leaving his dagger
and greatcoat in the cloakroom. He will also remove
his 'Schirmmütze' and gloves before taking his seat. The major
now appears in his walking out (or service) dress. Adopted
in July 1937 as an optional dress, the 'ornamented' tunic
is piped in the arm-of-service color around the dark
bluish-green collar, around the upper edge of the cuff turn
ups, and along the front panels, from the lower edge of the
skirt up to the top button. The tunic has five metal buttons
down the front. The four pockets - box pleated on the
chest and 'bellows' type on the skirt - have scalloped
flaps. Stitched near the shoulder seam and
buttoned near the collar, the shoulder straps
are made of bright aluminum interwoven braid
on a white cloth backing. The white collar
patches are adorned with bright aluminum
'Litzen' and a thin median braid
of the same material.

The breast
eagle is
embroidered
in bright
aluminum
thread
on a dark
bluish-green
overlay. The
ribbon bar
includes
the Iron Cross
2nd Class,
the 1941-42
Eastern Campaign
medal and the
medal for 12 years'
service
(a small gilded eagle
on a blue ribbon).
Pinned to the chest
are the Iron Cross 1st Class,
the Gold wound badge
and the Infantry general
assault badge awarded
for taking part in three
or more infantry assaults.
The cuff title is sewn
one centimeter above
the upper edge of the cuff
turn-up. All the buttons
are made of embossed metal
and finished in silver.

TANK BUSTER, NORMANDY

The green drill tunic has five buttons down the front but no lining, and its collar is secured by a hook. The four pleated pockets have pointed flaps. Made of dark bluish green serge, the collar has bright silver NCO braid. The collar tabs are woven of gray thread, and stitched on a facing cloth backing. They lack the arm-of-service color piping. The dark bluish green shoulder tabs also bear the silver NCO braid, they are piped in white for the infantry. The breast eagle is embroidered in white thread on a dark bluish-green backing.

The gas mask carrier strap is slung over the left shoulder. The assault pack and the canvas magazine pouches are suspended from the black leather belt and braces. A stick grenade is slipped into the belt; an egg-shaped grenade hangs by its loop from the left chest pocket button.

The smooth soled shoes are fitted with heel and toe cleats. Made of black leather, they are worn with web anklets. The shoes are laced through five holes and four black painted hooks at the top.

On 25 August 1944 at 9.30am, two weakened companies from the Heer's (Army) 346th Infantry Division were deployed in front of Epaignes, near Cormeilles in Normandy. A short while later, a recce unit from the British 49th Division ran into the German defense lines and was stopped dead in its tracks.

The field gray sidecap has no ventilation eyelets. The German national emblem, an eagle, is embroidered in gray thread on a brown backing; the black, white and red cockade is embroidered on a square piece of the same cloth. The tank destruction badge is sewn on the left sleeve. This badge shows the silhouette of tank, made of metal, affixed to a rectangular patch of silver thread piped in black.

The entrenching tool carrier is made of strong cardboard and black leather. The black leather 'Y' straps are black on one side and unfinished on the other. The '60' Panzerfaust is painted green with yellow stenciled markings.

The gas mask carrier has been sprayed brown and olive green on a dark yellow background. The reversible tent section has the same medium green and dark brown splinter camouflage pattern on both sides (one has a light field gray background the other and a dark gray-green one). The thin vertical stripes are medium green.

The camouflage smock is cut from light cotton material, with a fastening string at the waist. The sleeves are gathered at the wrist by a button and strap. A disruptive pattern of dark brown and green blotches with soft and hard edges stands out on the light tan background. Thin green stripes complete the camouflage effect. The smock is fitted with a hood but has no face veil; it is adjusted with a cord strung through seven button holes. There are two vertical slits concealed by a flap on the chest. The trousers have been theater-made cut from reclaimed tent section material, with the standard splinter pattern of light olive, brown and dark green blotches. The garment is held around the waist by a cord which slips through a hem. It has neither pockets nor fly.

The steel helmet is painted dark yellow blended with blurred dark green blotches. Chicken mesh has been added for affixing foliage. The national emblem on the left side has not been painted¾over.

77

ARTILLERY OFFICER, FALAISE POCKET

SMG Magazine pouches and a P-38 holster are fastened to the black leather belt. The 7 x 70 binoculars (fitted with a lens cover) are slung around the neck. The trousers are made of green drill. They have a fob pocket and their side slits have straight edges and no buttons. The fly has four buttons. The half belt is secured with a metal buckle. Eight dished metal buttons — the same as those for the fly — are stitched on the outer side of the waist to fasten the braces. The black leather ankle boots have seven pairs of eyelets each.

Falaise Pocket, 19-20 August 1944. This second lieutenant has managed to collect around him a few self-propelled guns - all that's left of the retreating batteries decimated in the terrible rearguard actions. Allied fighters rule the Normandy skies and, to keep out of their deadly sights, the armored vehicles hardly ever venture out of the protection of the hedgerows. From undercover, the artillerymen will pounce on the soldiers of the VII US Corps who have skirted Argentan to better hurry the Germans and prevent them from linking up with the 2nd SS Panzer Division at Saint-Lambert.

Originally finished in field gray, the helmet has been repainted dark green and fitted with chicken mesh for affixing camouflage. A captured French Army shirt, made of light olive poplin, is worn under the reed green drill short jacket of SP gun crews. The left panel of the double breasted garment is fastened with five synthetic buttons. The two vertical side slits have reinforced edges. The waist fastens with a drawstring. The tunic is unlined. The cuff slits, with a button near the lower edge, enable the soldier to roll up his sleeves. Stitched near the armhole seam, the shoulder straps are made of scarlet cloth (the self-propelled artillery branch color) and flat aluminum braid. The officer collar patches are made of dark bluish-green cloth, with silver 'tresse' and red piping. The chest eagle is embroidered in aluminum thread on a bluish-green backing.

The junior officer has now donned a soft 'Feldmütze alter Art' (older type field cap, introduced in 1934). Fitted with a black leather peak, the headgear is cut in fine field gray cloth, with a dark bluish-green band (introduced in June 1937). The crown and band are piped in red.

The Iron Cross 1st Class and '25 Class' General Assault Badge are pinned to the jacket.
The metal board holds maps and can be used to jot down messages.

Right.
Established in June 1943, the '25 Class' General Assault badge was awarded for taking part in 25 or more infantry assaults or spending 15 months on active duty.
The badge is cast in fine quality zinc; the laurel wreath made of nickel-copper alloy is finished in dull silver. Like the bottom device with the figure '25,' the eagle, stick grenade and eagle set is made of fine quality zinc and finished in dark gray.

Below.
Cut in sturdy gray-green cotton drill, the short, double-breasted jacket is identical to the model shown on the left but for the following difference: the garment has seven gray metal buttons down its right flap; the shoulder straps are secured with a loop at the armhole and a small button near the collar. Finally, the jacket has a large patch inner pocket on its left front.

The breeches are made of thick ribbed gray wool. The jackboots are made of black leather.

GROSSDEUTSCHLAND ENGINEER

Worn over a light gray jersey shirt, the tunic is made of gray cotton. Close fitting, it is unlined and devoid of inner pockets. The dark bluish-green collar is enhanced with silver braid around its edges. The tunic is done up with five buttons down the front and a collar hook. The four box pleated pockets (chest and skirt) seal with pointed button flaps.

All the tunic's buttons - including those of the shoulder tabs - are made of metal and painted field gray. Above the right chest pocket, the eagle is embroidered in white thread on a dark bluish-green backing. The Iron Cross 1st Class and General Assault badge are pinned to the left chest pocket.

The black leather belt is fitted with an aluminum buckle and supports the black leather P-38 holster.

In early 1944, the Großdeutschland Panzer Division notched up yet another success when it captured the town of Wilkowirshken in Latvia.

General Schörner, commanding Army Group 'North,' personally congratulated the victors, particularly the soldiers of the engineer battalion.

The 3-cm wide cuff title is piped in white and stitched 16.5 cm above the lower edge of the right cuff. The 'late-style' long hand lettering is embroidered in white thread.

Above.
The removable, early-type shoulder straps are made of dark bluish-green cloth. Enhanced with silver NCO braid around the edge, it has pinned-on rank stars in silver embossed metal and gilt 'GD' (Großdeutschland) cipher.

Right.
The senior NCO has donned his field gray cloth cap. The eagle in field gray thread and the national cockade are woven on a common trapezoidal backing. Woven in gray thread and piped in black (engineers), the early type collar tabs are stitched onto a dark bluish-green backing.

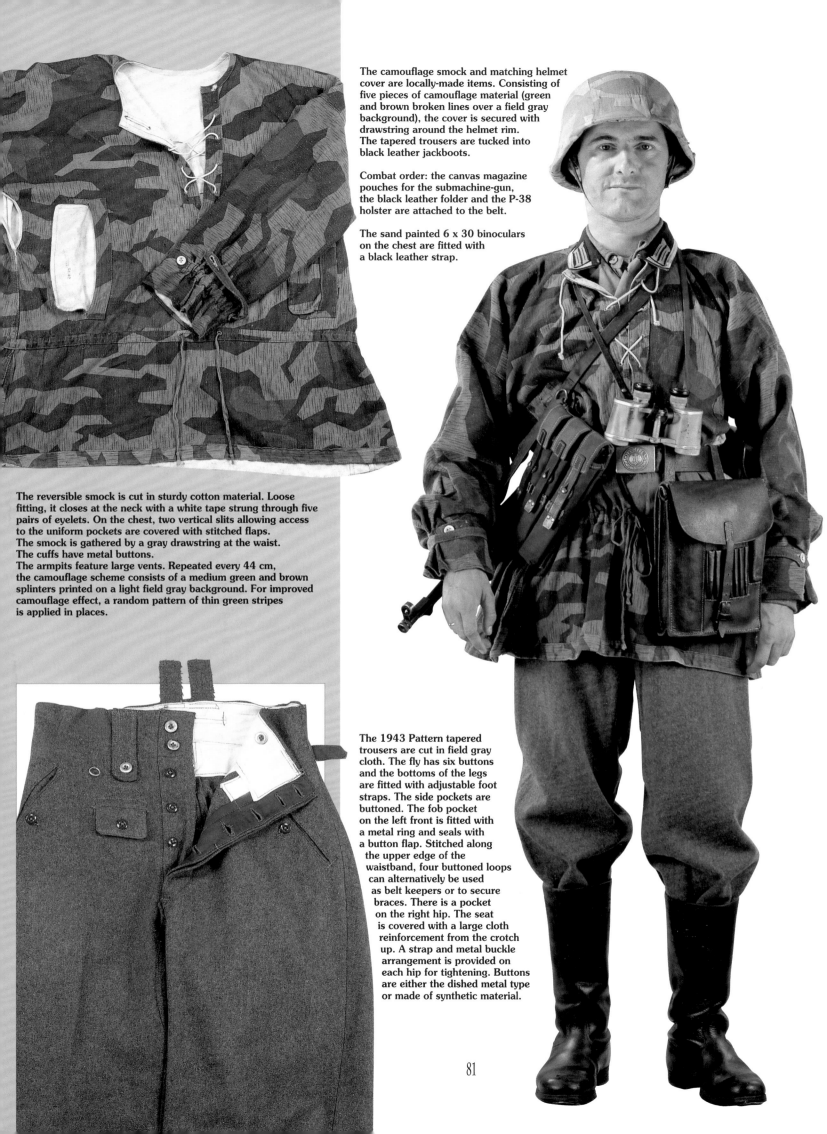

The camouflage smock and matching helmet cover are locally-made items. Consisting of five pieces of camouflage material (green and brown broken lines over a field gray background), the cover is secured with drawstring around the helmet rim. The tapered trousers are tucked into black leather jackboots.

Combat order: the canvas magazine pouches for the submachine-gun, the black leather folder and the P-38 holster are attached to the belt.

The sand painted 6 x 30 binoculars on the chest are fitted with a black leather strap.

The reversible smock is cut in sturdy cotton material. Loose fitting, it closes at the neck with a white tape strung through five pairs of eyelets. On the chest, two vertical slits allowing access to the uniform pockets are covered with stitched flaps. The smock is gathered by a gray drawstring at the waist. The cuffs have metal buttons. The armpits feature large vents. Repeated every 44 cm, the camouflage scheme consists of a medium green and brown splinters printed on a light field gray background. For improved camouflage effect, a random pattern of thin green stripes is applied in places.

The 1943 Pattern tapered trousers are cut in field gray cloth. The fly has six buttons and the bottoms of the legs are fitted with adjustable foot straps. The side pockets are buttoned. The fob pocket on the left front is fitted with a metal ring and seals with a button flap. Stitched along the upper edge of the waistband, four buttoned loops can alternatively be used as belt keepers or to secure braces. There is a pocket on the right hip. The seat is covered with a large cloth reinforcement from the crotch up. A strap and metal buckle arrangement is provided on each hip for tightening. Buttons are either the dished metal type or made of synthetic material.

81

PANZER CORPORAL, NORMANDY

The gray jersey shirt is done up with four cardboard buttons down the front. The chest pocket flaps have straight edges, and the cuffs have a button near the lower edge. The national emblem is woven in white thread on a black background. Stitched on a black patch, the corporal chevron are on the left sleeve. The Tank assault badge is pinned to the left pocket on two thread loops. This badge was awarded for taking part in three armored assaults on three different days.

Summer 1944. The armored column grinds to a stop by the edge of the forest lining a Normandy road. But the trees only afford sparse cover and the sun is already high... A few crewmen leap out of their PzKpfW IVs in shirtsleeve order although others are still wearing two-piece drill suits over the black uniforms.
Supported by a series of original photographs, these unusual fighting uniforms are the subject of this study.

The throat microphone is carried in the right trouser pocket. Its lead is slipped under the leather belt.

The corporal is wearing the other rank's black armored troops' cap. The small buttons fastening the turn-up have a black finish. The tricolor cockade and the eagle are woven in gray thread on a black underlay. The soldier has donned a denim two-piece suit over the black wool uniform and shirt. The picture clearly shows the two ways of doing up the jacket: the four green synthetic buttons were used for a tight fit, whereas the seven gray-green cardboard buttons were selected for a loose, more comfortable wear. The seven-button set extends up to the neck.

With its collar done up, the double-breasted short jacket closes in the same way and affords the same protection as the denim suit worn on top of it.

The short-shaft, black leather boots have cleated and studded soles.

The corporal is now clad in the 'Panzertruppen' protection suit cut in reed green canvas. The short, double-breasted jacket is done up over the right side with buttons covered by a fly front. The collar secures with a black metal hook. The large patch pocket on the left side of the chest has a three-pointed button flap. The cuff slits are done up with a button under tab.

The breast eagle is woven in gray thread on a field gray backing. Piped in pink - the branch color for German armored forces - the collar patches are made of black cloth and sport a silver death's head made of embossed metal. Also piped in pink and made of black cloth, the shoulder straps are secured with a loop on the armhole seam and a small field gray button near the collar.

There are large vents under the armpits. Two belt slits are provided at waist level. The garment is unlined and tightens with two drawstrings on the small of the back.

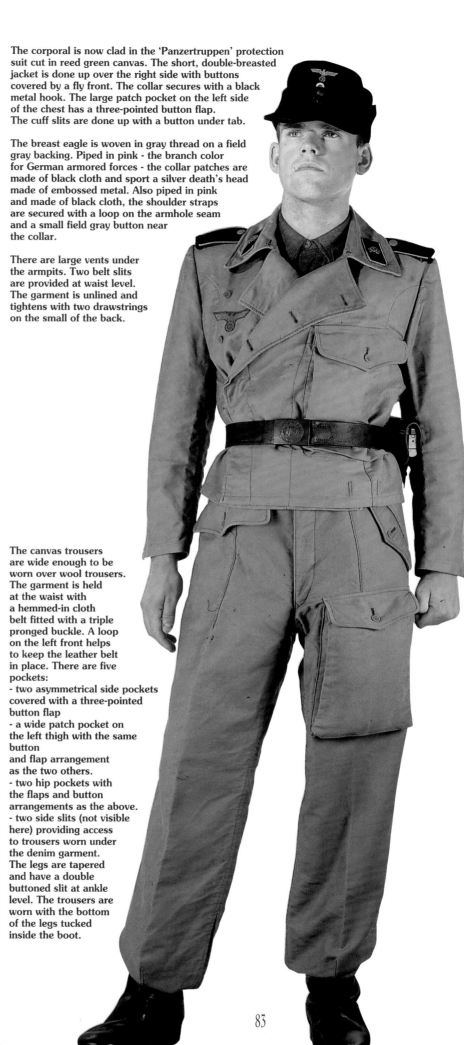

The canvas trousers are wide enough to be worn over wool trousers. The garment is held at the waist with a hemmed-in cloth belt fitted with a triple pronged buckle. A loop on the left front helps to keep the leather belt in place. There are five pockets:
- two asymmetrical side pockets covered with a three-pointed button flap
- a wide patch pocket on the left thigh with the same button and flap arrangement as the two others.
- two hip pockets with the flaps and button arrangements as the above.
- two side slits (not visible here) providing access to trousers worn under the denim garment. The legs are tapered and have a double buttoned slit at ankle level. The trousers are worn with the bottom of the legs tucked inside the boot.

The brown bakelite binocular case is carried on the belt along with the entrenching tool, stick grenade and the magazine pouch. The gas mask carrier strap is slung over the right shoulder.

SQUAD LEADER, NORMANDY

The NCO wears the 'reed green' drill uniform. The tunic shares the characteristics of the field gray wool garment. It is done up with six pebbled metal buttons down the front; the pockets have pointed flaps.

The straight matching trousers have a fob patch pocket on the right front. The side pockets have straight edges and no flaps. Kept up with braces, they are tightened with a pronged buckle and strap on both hips. The small metal buttons are the dished type.

The regulation field lamp is secured by a short tab to the shoulder strap button.

On 9 June 1944, the grenadiers of the 916th Infantry Regiment, 352nd Infantry Division, were locked in fierce combat with the GIs of the 2nd US Infantry Division.

Firmly entrenched, the Germans were holding the Béri-gny-Saint-Georges-d'Elle sector to the south-west of the Cerisy forest. Making the most of the terrain which lent itself remarkably well to defensive warfare, the Eastern Front veterans checked every move the Americans made to break through their lines and advance towards the south.

Above.
The 1943 Pattern 'Feldmütze' bears the standard woven insignia - gray eagle and tricolor cockade - on a single trapezoidal backing. The NCO silver braiding is stitched around the edge of the collar. The late-type 'Litzen' (collar patches) are stitched on the plain gray-green collar. The field gray shoulder tabs are piped in white, the infantry service color. The rank is indicated by the silver braiding and star. Woven in gray thread on a field gray backing, the chest eagle is stitched with beige thread above the right chest pocket. The tunic is worn over a gray jersey shirt (pocket less model with pressed cardboard buttons).

Left.
Used for affixing foliage, the chicken mesh is secured to the helmet with a length of wire running around the shell and hooked to the left and right sides of the rim. The poncho/tent section has a central vent for the head.

84

The NCO has donned the reversible 'Zeltbahn,' a triangular multipurpose camouflage poncho intended to be worn as a rain cape or rigged with others to form a shelter. The individual equipment is strapped over the tent section, with the entrenching tool carrier fastened to the belt. The trousers legs are gathered in canvas anklets securing with two leather straps. The ankle boots have retained their natural leather color.

Right.
The entrenching tool carrier is secured to the belt (the pistol holster is carried on the left side but not seen here), along with the bread bag to which the water bottle and mess tin are hooked. The antigas cape is wrapped around the gasmask container and fastened with cloth tape. In fighting order, the gasmask strap is slung over the left shoulder.

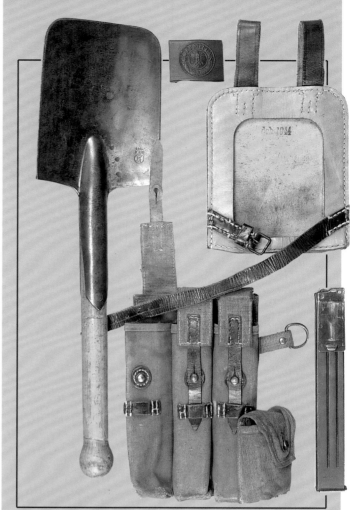

Above.
Fastened to the belt with a wide leather loop, the entrenching tool carrier is made of sand color, varnished cardboard 'Preßstoff.' One end of the carrier strap is longer so it can be used to secure together the bayonet scabbard and the handle of the entrenching tool. Made of canvas, the left-hand side pouch holds three submachine-gun magazines and has a small pocket on the side for the magazine loading tool.

The artillery NCO operates a range-finder. He has an early pattern sidecap in field gray wool, and a locally made shirt, made of tent section material.

21ST PZ. DIV. GUNNER, NORMANDY

Early on 6 June 1944, the 21st Panzer Division rumbled out of its barracks near Caen to muster in the Chicheboville woods and around Virlont to confront the British 3rd Infantry Division.

For several weeks, the German defenders stubbornly denied British forces access to Caen. Now serving with the 2nd Group, 155th Armored Artillery Regiment, this man is an Africa Campaign veteran who belongs to the crew of a self-propelled 105-mm gun.

Below.
Initially meant for assault gun crews, the short, double-breasted jacket was made of field gray cloth and widely issued to personnel of the 155th Armored Artillery Regiment. The garment is done up with the left panel overlapping the seven buttons on the right. The deep inner pocket on the left and the lining are made of gray-green sateen. The jacket is tightened with a drawstring at the waist. To roll up the sleeves more easily, a slit with two buttons runs down from the elbow. Piped in red - the artillery branch color - the field gray shoulder straps are secured by a loop on the armhole seam and a button near the collar. Also piped in scarlet, the bluish-green collar patches are made of facing cloth. Woven in dull gray thread on a pale green underlay, the eagle is stitched to the right chest between the fifth and sixth buttons.

Above.
The 'Heeres Flakabzeichen' (Anti-Aircraft War Badge) was instituted by the German High Command in July 1941. The badge was awarded to gun crews, sound locators and searchlight operators. Designed by Wilhelm Ernest Peekhaus of Berlin and finely cast in zinc, the badge consists of an upward pointing 88-mm gun, girded with oak leaves and capped with an imperial eagle clutching a swastika.

Introduced on 15 January 1943 for Heer personnel, the 'Afrika' cuff title can be regarded as a medal in its own right. The criteria for award were:
– four months' duties for the soldiers deployed during the May 1943 Tunisia campaign.
– six months' duties in North Africa.
– contracting an illness or suffering a wound resulting in permanent incapacity to serve in this theater.
– awarded automatically to the recipient of any medal for bravery.
The cuff title is made of brushed cotton tape, 33-mm wide, with embroidered silver-gray lettering and palm trees. The title is edged at the top and bottom with a band of silver embroidery. Several variants were observed.

The helmet has received several coats of tan and brown paint. The regulation gray jersey shirt is worn with a black tie. The Heer Flak insignia pinned on the chest shows that the gunner has served with distinction. The 'Afrika' title is stitched on the bottom of the left sleeve 14.5 cm above the lower edge. The rank chevrons on the left sleeve are stitched on a field gray backing. A canvas SMG magazine pouch and a P-08 holster are fastened to the black leather belt fitted with a field gray steel buckle.

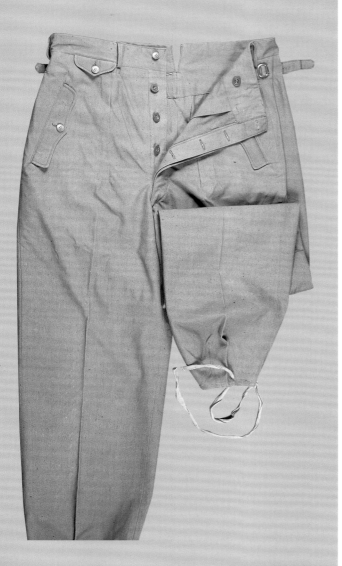

The field gray wool trousers are similar in cut and design to those of the figure at left.

The black leather boots secure with four pairs of eyelets and three pairs of hooks.

Left.
The trousers are made of gray canvas. They are kept up by braces or alternatively fastened with a belt. The slanted side pockets have pointed button flaps. Under the belt band on the left front is a fob pocket sealing with a button flap. There is a pronged buckle arrangement on both hips to tighten the waist. The fly has five dished synthetic buttons. The other buttons are made of brown synthetic material. The tapered legs tighten with two tapes and a button.

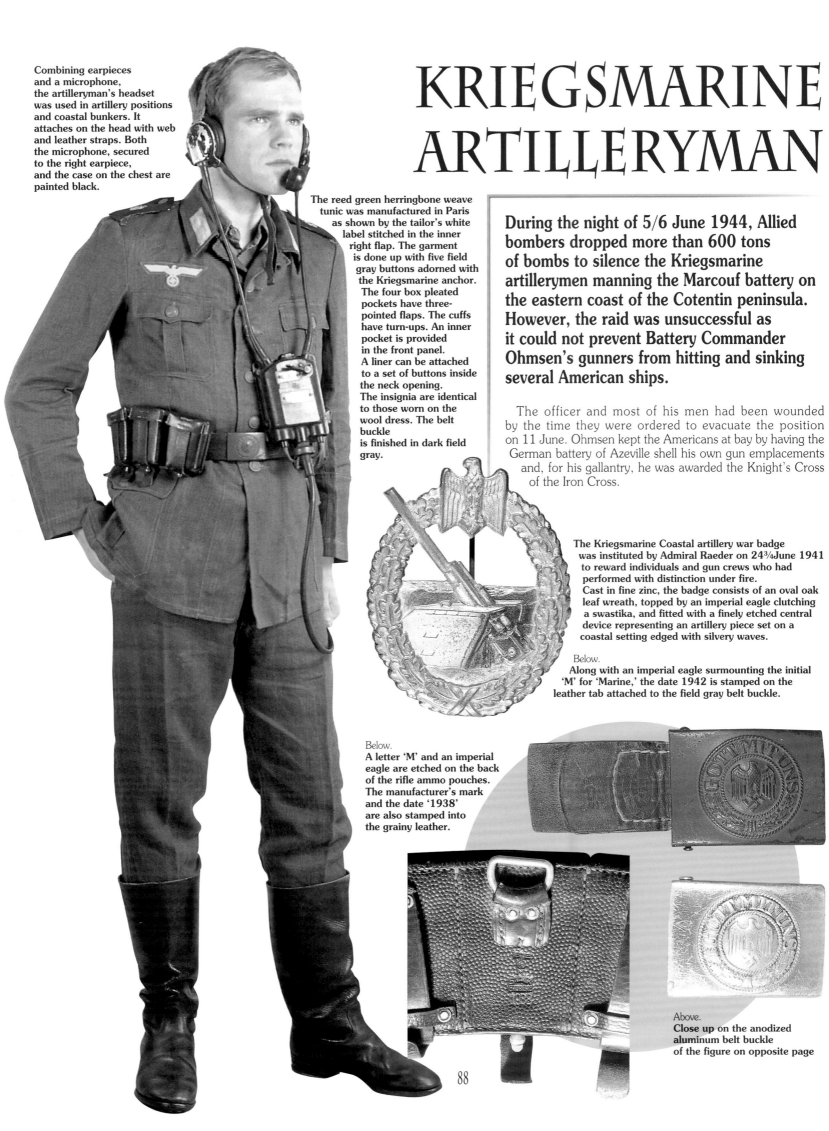

Combining earpieces and a microphone, the artilleryman's headset was used in artillery positions and coastal bunkers. It attaches on the head with web and leather straps. Both the microphone, secured to the right earpiece, and the case on the chest are painted black.

KRIEGSMARINE ARTILLERYMAN

The reed green herringbone weave tunic was manufactured in Paris as shown by the tailor's white label stitched in the inner right flap. The garment is done up with five field gray buttons adorned with the Kriegsmarine anchor. The four box pleated pockets have three-pointed flaps. The cuffs have turn-ups. An inner pocket is provided in the front panel. A liner can be attached to a set of buttons inside the neck opening. The insignia are identical to those worn on the wool dress. The belt buckle is finished in dark field gray.

During the night of 5/6 June 1944, Allied bombers dropped more than 600 tons of bombs to silence the Kriegsmarine artillerymen manning the Marcouf battery on the eastern coast of the Cotentin peninsula. However, the raid was unsuccessful as it could not prevent Battery Commander Ohmsen's gunners from hitting and sinking several American ships.

The officer and most of his men had been wounded by the time they were ordered to evacuate the position on 11 June. Ohmsen kept the Americans at bay by having the German battery of Azeville shell his own gun emplacements and, for his gallantry, he was awarded the Knight's Cross of the Iron Cross.

The Kriegsmarine Coastal artillery war badge was instituted by Admiral Raeder on 24¾June 1941 to reward individuals and gun crews who had performed with distinction under fire. Cast in fine zinc, the badge consists of an oval oak leaf wreath, topped by an imperial eagle clutching a swastika, and fitted with a finely etched central device representing an artillery piece set on a coastal setting edged with silvery waves.

Below.
Along with an imperial eagle surmounting the initial 'M' for 'Marine,' the date 1942 is stamped on the leather tab attached to the field gray belt buckle.

Below.
A letter 'M' and an imperial eagle are etched on the back of the rifle ammo pouches. The manufacturer's mark and the date '1938' are also stamped into the grainy leather.

Above.
Close up on the anodized aluminum belt buckle of the figure on opposite page

The shoulder straps are made of bluish-green wool cloth which have pointed ends and no piping. The coastal artillery insignia, an anchor overlaid with a winged shell, is embroidered in bright yellow thread.

The collar patches are woven in gray thread and feature a thin golden yellow piping down the middle. The chest eagle is woven in golden yellow thread on a green backing. The field gray metal buttons are adorned with the Kriegsmarine fouled anchor.

The helmet is camouflaged with gray-green and dark yellow blurred patches. On the left side, the imperial eagle on a black shield is finished in the golden yellow service color of the Kriegsmarine. The chin strap is made of brown leather.

The tunic is made of field gray cloth. It has five buttons down the front, a collar hook and four box pleated pockets with pointed flaps. On the small of the back, three belt hooks protrude from by oversewn eyelets. A vent with overlapping flaps runs down the back of the skirt and two adjustable darts are provided at kidney level. The artilleryman sports medal ribbon of the 1 October 1938 'Sudetenland' commemorative medal.

The gilt anodized aluminum belt buckle was issued to Kriegsmarine other ranks. The matching trousers are tucked into black leather jackboots. The weapon is a K-98k rifle.

The seaman trousers are made in the same material as the drill tunic. The rectangular front flap could be fastened with four buttons. There is a side pockets on the right and a double pocket arrangement on the left. The legs are slightly tapered and gathered with a tab on metal buttons.

THE 17TH LUFTWAFFE FIELD DIVISION

Normandy Front, 17 August 1944: commanded by General H.K. Höcker, the 17th Luftwaffe Field Division is taking up positions to the south of the Eure river. Its mission is to hold back the XIX US Corps until the bulk of the retreating German forces have crossed the Seine

Below.
The Luftwaffe eagle, the brown and green camouflage finish and the net hooks are clearly shown on this left view of the helmet.

Shown in full combat order, this artilleryman belongs to the 1st Group, 20th Flak Regiment, a unit attached to the 17th Division. The regulation blue-gray 'Fliegerbluse' is worn under the Luftwaffe splinter camouflage smock (sharp edged green and brown pattern over a field gray background). The cotton garment is done up with five gray-blue synthetic buttons. The unlined smock has a large inner pocket on the left side. The shoulder straps are made of matching cloth. The cuffs are fastened with straps and metal buttons. The side pockets have large straight-edged button flaps. The imperial eagle on the chest is woven in gray thread on a blue-gray backing.

90

Left, and bottom left.
The camouflage net is secured to the helmet with two steel hooks fastened to the liner. When lowered, the net covers the face. When raised and hooked to the rim of the helmet, the camouflage net helps to disrupt the shape of the head.

Right.
Like the bayonet frog, the suspension straps and K-98k ammunition pouches are made of brown leather. Cut in blue-gray wool material, the trousers are kept up with braces and fasten at the back with a strap and buckle. They have two side pockets, two hip pockets and a small fob pocket on the front.

The leg bottoms are gathered in blue-gray canvas anklets reinforced with brown leather.

Brown leather boots with seven pairs of eyelets.

(© D. Lodieu/Batailles 2004)

Above.
The gas cape is secured to the gasmask carrier with two black leather straps. The bread bag and the water bottle felt cover are the same typical color with only the mess tin being finished in green.

Left.
The gray-blue 'Fliegerbluse' is fly fronted. The flaps of the two slanted skirt pockets close with convex buttons. The cuffs are fastened with a strap buttoning on the inside. Like the shoulder tabs, the collar patches are piped in scarlet (the service color of the artillery). The three dull metal wings on the collar patches indicate the rang of corporal. The chest eagle is woven in gray thread. The brown leather belt is fitted with a buckle finished in flat dark blue-gray. The 'Heer Flak Insignia' is pinned on the left chest.

Normandy, July 1944. A Flak artilleryman hides the gun under branches on the road side.

DEFENCE OF THE REICH FIGHTER PILOT

The leather flying jacket bears the following insignia: second-lieutenant shoulder straps, metal eagle on the right, Iron Cross 1st Class and pilot badge on the left. A compass and a holster for the 6.35 mm pistol are attached to the brown leather belt which tightens with a double-pronged metal buckle.

To bring Hitler's Third Reich to its knees, the Allied air forces carried out massive bombing raids on major German cities. The pilots of the 'Richthofen' Squadron doggedly fought on until the very end to save their country from total destruction.

The flying helmet top is made of light, mesh-type material, reinforced with a black leather strip. Black leather is used for the rest of the headgear. The built-in headphones are protected with brown leather cups. The lead plug is secured to the back. The oxygen mask (left in the aircraft) is secured with a steel hook on the cheeks. The throat microphone is held in place with two rigid black leather straps. The life preserver is made of yellow rubberized material and secured with three metal pronged buckles. Inflation is achieved by using the compressed gas bottle carried in a small pocket at the bottom of the left panel. In case of emergency, the preserver can be inflated by blowing through the tube on the upper left. The black leather gloves are tightened with a pressure stud and strap.

Left.
Made of gray blue cotton, the flying trousers are lined with gray-blue synthetic fur. Braces and hemmed-in belt around the waist are used to keep the garment up. The zipped fly is reinforced with a two-button strap at the top. The trousers legs are secured with zips down the inner side of the ankles. The small leather tabs on the knees cover the plugs connecting to the aircraft heating system leads

93

DEFENCE OF THE REICH FIGHTER PILOT

Officer pattern 1943 Luftwaffe field cap, with silver crown piping and embroidered eagle insignia.
The turn-up is fastened with one silver button.

The privately purchased leather jacket was a favorite among fighter pilots. This one has four pockets closed with zips or buttoned flaps. The jacket is done up with a zip down the front and a buckle and strap at the waist.

Lined with synthetic fur, the black boots have suede tops and rubber soles. Tightening is achieved with buckled straps at the top and on the instep. For a tighter fit, the boots have zips down the inner sides and tabs on the inside top.

The pilot had his picture taken before another mission. In this photograph, he wears full service dress with stiff peaked cap.

94

The successful pilot has now been promoted to the rank of captain as the two stars adorning his shoulder tabs indicate. He is clad in the blue-gray wool service with matching officer's sidecap. Worn with an open collar, the 'Fliegerbluse' short jacket is fly fronted. On the lapels, the rank insignia are embroidered in silver bullion on a yellow underlay (yellow was the service color of flying personnel). The collar piping and the chest eagle are also made of silver bullion. Sewn to the right sleeve, the cuff title is made of blue cotton and carries the 'JAGDGESCHWADER RICHTHOFEN' inscription embroidered in gray thread.

The following awards are worn on the right side of the chest: the Iron Cross 1st Class, the Pilot Badge in bullion version and the Silver wound badge. Above, these is the Silver class day fighter operational flying clasp awarded for 60 missions. The German cross in gold (bullion version) in worn on the right side of the chest under the eagle. The Iron Cross 2nd Class ribbon is stitched through the second buttonhole. The pilot has been awarded the Knight's Cross and wears the prestigious award around the neck. A brown leather belt, fine gray leather gloves, gray-blue wool breeches and high boots complete the uniform.

Displayed on the leather flying jacket are the flying gloves, dress gloves, sidecap, stiff peaked cap, flying headgear, compass, gravity knife, JG2 (Jagdgeschwader 2) cuff title and flare pistol.

Previous page.

1. Sealing with a pressure stud flap, the large pocket on the left thigh holds the flare pistol (secured with a long strap to the inner side of the pocket) and the knife as well as the lead and plugs connecting to the heating system.
2. Zipped vertical pockets holding a square compressed gas bottle for the life preserver.

3. Thigh pocket, sealing with a pressure stud flap and fitted with adjustable straps to secure maps and pistol flares.
4. Vertical zipped pocket.
5. Triangular pocket with pressure stud tabs to secure the handgun.
6. Vertical pocket holding the yellow box for the identification flag; sealing with a pressure stud flap.

RECONNAISSANCE UNIT OFFICER, ITALY

Both the helmet cover and jacket have been locally made from tent section material.

Strapped around the helmet, the goggles have been borrowed from one of the group's motorcyclists. They are secured with an elasticized strap and adjust on the front between the lenses with a small bolt and nut. The metal fittings are painted gray and the eyepieces molded in gray rubber.

The short jacket is done up with a zip down the front. The shoulder area is reinforced with a yoke. The cuffs are gathered with pointed tabs fastening on dished buttons. The jacket is gathered around the waist; there is an inner patch pocket in the left panel. Both a shirt and the short black double-breasted jacket of armored crews are worn under the camouflage jacket.

The pistol holster is fastened to an officer's black leather belt with two-pronged buckle.

The green drill trouser legs are gathered around the ankles. The leather boots have seven pair of eyelets each.

The radio operator's voice sounded almost surreal as the message transmitted by one of the group's advanced elements reached the HQ of Pz. Aufkl. Abt. 26:

"They are now in the valley, with armor, trucks and artillery. Their vanguard is now entering the gutted village. They will reach the bridge in a few minutes. They are heading right in your direction!" From atop their rocky observation post, the men of the recce group were closely monitoring the advance of the enemy through their binoculars. This was early May 1944 on the Italian front somewhere between Frosisone and Velletri. Their mission over, the men of the recce detachment briskly pulled out as the artillerymen of Panzer. Art. Rgt. 93 of 26th Panzer Division were already training their guns at the valley.

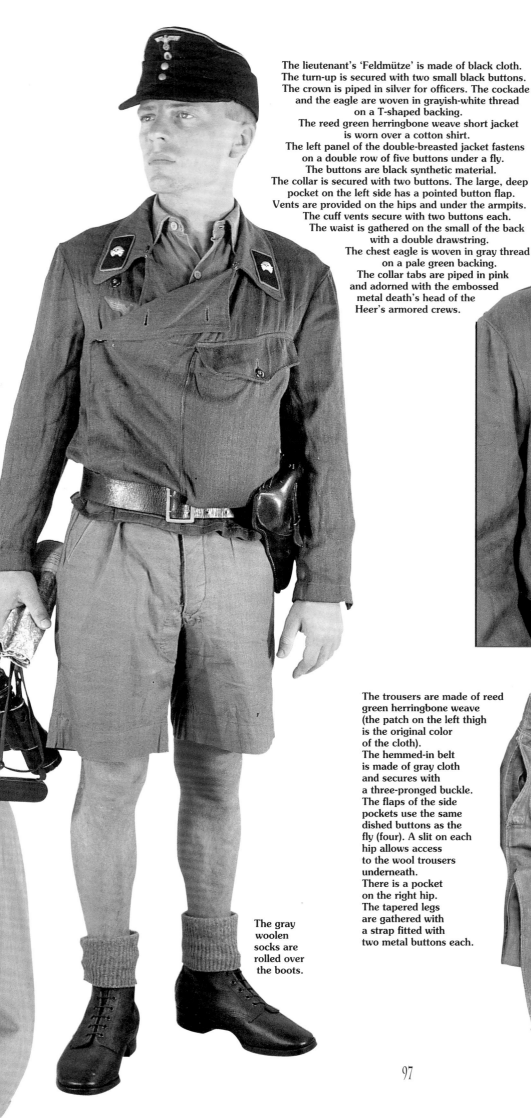

The lieutenant's 'Feldmütze' is made of black cloth. The turn-up is secured with two small black buttons. The crown is piped in silver for officers. The cockade and the eagle are woven in grayish-white thread on a T-shaped backing.
The reed green herringbone weave short jacket is worn over a cotton shirt.
The left panel of the double-breasted jacket fastens on a double row of five buttons under a fly. The buttons are black synthetic material.
The collar is secured with two buttons. The large, deep pocket on the left side has a pointed button flap. Vents are provided on the hips and under the armpits. The cuff vents secure with two buttons each. The waist is gathered on the small of the back with a double drawstring.
The chest eagle is woven in gray thread on a pale green backing.
The collar tabs are piped in pink and adorned with the embossed metal death's head of the Heer's armored crews.

The gray woolen socks are rolled over the boots.

The trousers are made of reed green herringbone weave (the patch on the left thigh is the original color of the cloth).
The hemmed-in belt is made of gray cloth and secures with a three-pronged buckle. The flaps of the side pockets use the same dished buttons as the fly (four). A slit on each hip allows access to the wool trousers underneath. There is a pocket on the right hip. The tapered legs are gathered with a strap fitted with two metal buttons each.

97

'LANGEMARCK' CADET OFFICER

The double-breasted parka is done up with a double set of five buttons. The garment is gathered with a hemmed-in belt at the waist and a drawstring at the neck. The cuffs are tightened with button straps. The elbows bear cloth reinforcement patches. The inner pockets have pointed flaps. The hood can be lowered and folded around the neck for protection against the cold. The buttons are made of metal or cardboard.

Two stick grenades and a set of magazine pouches are fastened to the black leather belt fitted with a large double pronged buckle. The P-08 holster is not visible in the picture.

The gray gloves are knitted in wool.

The field gray breeches have zippers on the ankles. Kept up with braces, they feature two flapless button pockets, one fob pocket and one hip pocket. The buttons are either made of cardboard or metal (dished type). The waist adjusts with a strap and pronged buckle arrangement on the back.

Intended for extreme weather, the high boots have leather shafts securing near the top with buckles and straps.

A volunteer with the SS 'Nordwest' Regiment at the time when Germany turned against Russia in 1941, this veteran has served as an NCO with the SS 'Flandern' Legion (Flemish Legion) on the Eastern Front. In this study, he has just graduated as a 'Standartenoberjunker' (cadet officer) from the Waffen-SS Academy before commissioning in the Flemish 6th 'Langemarck' Assault Brigade in February 1944.

The cuff title is stitched 14.5 cm above the bottom edge of the left sleeve. The inscription on the other ranks' title is woven in silver silk on a black background. The piping is done in aluminum thread.

Made of printed material, the reversible helmet cover is worn here with its brown side out. It is kept in place with three burnished metal spring-loaded, double-sided hooks (one on either side and one at the back) while the visor fits into a gusset. Like the helmet cover, the parka is worn with its brown side out. The unlined hood is made of the same material but its camouflage colors are more subdued.

The rank insignia of the future subaltern are displayed on the tunic shown on the left. On the right lapel is the black patch bordered with aluminum braid and struck with the twin silver embroidered runes. The left-hand patch has the senior WO rank insignia (two stars and aluminum braid with a thin black strip down the middle). The 'Hauptscharführer's' shoulder straps are made of black cloth piped in white (for the infantry).

The steel helmet is painted field gray; the left side decal represents the runes on a silver shield. The sleeve eagle is embroidered in gray thread on a black backing. Pinned to the left side, the ribbon bar includes the Iron Cross 2nd Class, War merit cross 2nd Class with swords and the medal for the 1941-42 Winter campaign in Russia. The Infantry assault badge is displayed on the left pocket. Worn over the left hip, the P-08 holster is slid on to the black leather belt.

The other ranks' field gray tunic is done up with five buttons down the front and a collar hook. The pockets have pointed flaps. The shoulder straps are stitched onto the armhole seam and buttoned near the collar. Initially finished in flat field gray, the buttons have become shiny with extensive wear.

Representing a rampant lion on a yellow backing, the Flemish Legion shield is woven in cotton thread.

The lack of a tie shows that the NCO is off duty. Wearing a light gray jersey shirt, the cadet has donned a 'Feldmütze alter Art' (early type cap), a soft, light headgear devoid of cords and stiffener. The peak is made of soft black leather. An embossed metal death's head is pinned at the front on the black velvet cap band piped in white. Made of field gray 'Döskin' cloth, the top is also piped in white. The death's head and the eagle are secured with prongs.

'VON SALZA' NCO, NARVA

The gray-green shirt is worn with a black tie. The short double breasted jacket features a wide collar and rounded lapels. The left panel fastens with seven black buttons. The cuff slits are buttoned. A deep pocket is provided in the black sateen lining in the left front. The shoulder straps are of black cloth, piped in pink (the armored force color), with silver NCO braid around the edge. The silver rank stars and figure '11' are made of silver finished metal. The right and left parallelogram-shaped collar tabs bear the SS runes woven in silver thread and the gray metal rank stars. The sleeve eagle is embroidered in white thread on a black backing.

The cuff title is stitched 14.5 cm above the lower edge of the sleeve. The ribbons of the Iron Cross 2d Class and the 1941-42 Russian Campaign are stitched through the second buttonhole. The Iron Cross 1st Class and the Armored force combat badge are pinned to the left side of the chest.

The regulation gloves are knitted in gray wool. The black leather shoes are cleated and studded.

Right.
The 'Oberscharführer' wears the black wool sidecap issued to Waffen-SS other ranks of armored units. Woven in dull gray thread, the death's head stitched to the front of the turn-up has taken on a yellowish hue with age. Woven in dull gray thread on a black backing, the Waffen-SS pattern eagle is smaller than that worn on the left sleeve. The cap is lined with black cloth.

Early 1944: after a grueling two-week retreat, the IIIrd German Corps units led by SS-Obergruppenführer (lieutenant-general) Felix Steiner reached the city of Narva in Estonia.

Although severely pressed, the Germans turned this sector into a bulwark to stem the Soviet steamroller. The city and the defensive positions were soon heavily shelled by the Russians who launched numerous assaults at the stronghold. Among the defenders were the tank crews of SS-Panzer. Abt. 11 'Hermann von Salza' ('Nordland' Panzer Division) who particularly distinguished themselves by repelling a powerful Russian thrust against the southern sector of the city on 11 February. In this action, the tank crews fought on as infantrymen after losing all their tanks. In early March, one of the battalion's Panther companies confronted and defeated a large number of T-34s in a series of epic duels.

Manufactured by BeVo of Wuppertal-Barmen, the 1943 Pattern cuff title is woven in black and gray silk. It was worn by all armored battalion personnel. The battalion took the name of Hermann von Salza (1211-39) a Grand Master of the Teutonic order.

100

ID tag for a warrant officer in the SS-Panzer-Abt. 11 'Hermann von Salza.' Worn around the neck from a thin cord, the aluminum tag caries the following inscriptions: '4./SS-PZ. RGT.11' indicating that the man belongs to the 4th Company, 11th Armored Regiment. 857 is the man's own number. Due to critical shortage of manpower, the regiment could never be expanded into the two-battalion formation it was initially meant to be. Instead, the unit remained a tank battalion, led by Sturmbannführer (major) Albert Kausch who was awarded the Knight's Cross on 28 August 1944

The black 1943 'Feldmütze' is made of thick black cloth and lined with gray sateen. The ¾ turn-up is kept up with two black painted buttons. Woven in dull gray thread on a black backing, the death's head badge is stitched to the front. The SS-pattern eagle appears on the left side.

A green scarf is worn under the wide collar. The sheepskin three-quarter length coat has a wide collar that can be kept up with a buttoned tab. Its integral hood is lined with white wool. The front and side pockets close with wooden toggles and black leather loops.

Below.
The trousers are cut in black wool cloth. The texture of this material is finer than the jacket's, even though both were issued to the same man. The trousers fasten around the waist with a belt slipped through seven loops. There is a fob pocket on the right front; the fly is done up with four buttons. The waist is done up with two buttons at the front and adjusts with a buckle and strap on each hip. The ¾ side pockets have vertical openings and seal with two-button flaps. The right hip pocket has a three-pointed buttoned flap. The buttons are made of black synthetic material. The seat is reinforced with cloth from the crotch up. The lower part of the tapered legs are lined with white cloth and gathered with drawstrings. The upper part of the trousers and the fly are lined with white cotton. The same material is used for the pockets.

Left.
Two types of cloth are used for the winter trousers worn by the soldier at right: thick gray-green cloth and white material. The garment is kept up with braces and adjusts with a double drawstring on the small of the back. The fly has four black synthetic buttons. The side pockets are buttoned. The legs are gathered with drawstrings at the ¾ ankle.

'BRANDENBURG' DIVISION OFFICER

The tunic is made of olive green captured Russian material. The garment is done up with six buttons down the front. The sleeves have turn-ups.

The shoulder straps are piped in light green (branch color of the 'Jäger') with double U-shaped aluminum braiding. The collar tabs are the same dark bluish-green color as the collar and adorned with a double gray thread braiding with green piping. The chest eagle is made of aluminum bullion set on a bluish-green underlay. The 'Jäger' oval badge - introduced in October 1943 - is worn on the right sleeve. The Iron Cross 1st Class and Infantry combat badge are pinned to the left chest pocket.

The brown leather holster for a 7.65 mm handgun is carried on a captured Russian belt. The belt was probably taken as a souvenir during a deep foray behind enemy lines (often wearing Red Army uniforms).

Cut in khaki cotton, the breeches are tucked into black leather riding boots.

After being involved in a ruthless struggle against the Dalmatian partisans throughout spring 1944, the men of the 'Brandenburg' Division relinquished the surprise raids and anti-guerilla sweeps to take part in Operation 'Rösselsprung.'

Refined by the 2nd Armored Army headquarters, the aim of this mission was to capture the city of Dvar in Yugoslavia where Marshall Tito had set up his command post. The men of the 1st Regiment were set at the spearhead of this action and, although they seized the city, the Germans failed to capture the guerilla leader. In the process they incurred severe losses as the partisan forces in the area numbered no fewer than six divisions.

Right.
Spring-summer 1944 in Northern Dalmatia. Manufactured in 1944, the 1943 Pattern 'Feldmütze' worn by this officer is cut in thick olive green cloth. This example bears the same metal eagle and cockade as used on the 'Schirmmütze'. The 'Jäger' (light infantry) oak leaf badge is pinned on the left side. The top has two pairs of metal ventilation grommets.

The 1942 Pattern helmet is finished in field gray. It has no insignia.

The tunic is cut in tent section material, camouflaged in the standard green, brown and field gray 'splinter' pattern. It has four buttons down the front, the box pleated pockets have pointed flaps. The collar is cut in dark bluish-green facing cloth. The chest eagle is woven in aluminum thread on a triangular, bluish-green backing. The officer has promoted to the rank of 'Oberleutnant' (lieutenant) as shown by the rank insignia stitched to the left sleeve. Rank marks for special garments are woven in green thread on a rectangular black backing. The submachine-gun pouches are fastened to the captured Russian belt.

Right.

The 'Brandenburg' cuff title was established in September 1944 when the survivors of the Abwehr special units (except the coastal defense units and the paratroopers) were commissioned into the 'Brandenburg' Panzer Grenadier Division. The unit was combat ready by mid-December 1944 and based in eastern Prussia. Worn on the left sleeve, the cuff title is made of thick dark green cloth. Lettering and piping are silver-gray.

A. Cap badge for 'Jäger' units.
The Heer 'Jäger' sleeve badge was worn for some time by the Abwehr's special units. These insignia were available in several variants, all of which retained the dark green backing. Sizes also differed, whether the insignia were embroidered (B, D and F) or woven (C and E). Some patterns had a wool cloth backing. The set shown here is not comprehensive.

103

7TH SS DIVISION MOUNTAIN RIFLEMAN

Worn over a gray jersey shirt, the tunic is made of field gray cloth and seals with five buttons down the front. The chest patch pockets and the skirt 'bellows' pockets have pointed flaps. The cuff slits are fastened with two gray synthetic buttons.

The belt is held in place by metal hooks protruding at waist level from oversewn eyelets at the front and back of the tunic. The collar secures with a hook. The metal buttons are finished in field gray. Issued in 1942, the tunic is lined with gray sateen, the same material is used for the field dressing pocket in the inner right panel. The mountain rifleman has been awarded the 'Infanterie Sturmabzeichen' for taking part in three assaults on three different days. The badge is pinned to the left chest pocket.

The ammunition pouches and the belt are made of black leather. The belt buckle is painted field gray.

Right.
The 'Feldmütze' is cut in field gray cloth. The turn-up is fastened with a button of beige synthetic material. Woven in gray thread on a black backing, the Waffen-SS death's head and eagle appear on the front. The mountain troops' edelweiss badge is stitched to the left ¾ side.

Commanded by SS-Brigadeführer (lieutenant-general) Carl Reichsrichter von Oberkamp, the 'Prinz Eugen' Division was involved in a massive sweep against Marshall Tito's 16th, 17th and 36th Proletarian brigades from 26 April to 5 May 1945.

The action took place in the Dinaric Alps, to the north-east of Sarajevo. The soldier depicted in this study belongs to the 8th Company, N°13 Regiment.

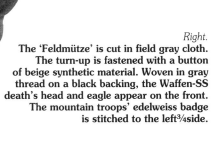

The 7th SS division took the name of François Eugene of Savoy-Carignan (1663-1736) a Paris-born Austrian general who expelled the Turks from Hungary and captured Belgrade in 1717. The cuff title is made of finely woven black tape adorned with silver gray lettering and aluminum thread piping. The title is stitched to the left sleeve, 14.5¾cm above the edge of the cuff.

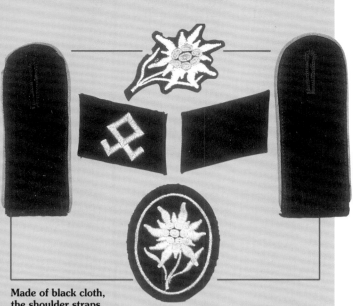

Made of black cloth, the shoulder straps are piped in green (which became the service color of Waffen-SS mountain formations in September 1943). The 'edelweiss' badge is both apparent on the cap (top), and as an oval sleeve badge on the right sleeve. Introduced in September 1943, this insignia is embroidered in silver-gray thread enhanced with gold and lemon yellow thread on a black backing. Also embroidered with silver gray thread on a black background, the 7th SS Division's collar patch insignia is the 'O' rune, the 23rd letter in the ancient Germanic alphabet. The other ranks' left collar tab was left in plain black cloth.

The camouflage pattern of the 'Tarnjacke' reversible smock consists of green, tan and brown blurred blotches interspersed on a pale green backing.
The garment is fitted with an elasticized band around the collar (missing here). The vertical chest opening secures with a lace strung through 10 oversewn eyelets. Giving the wearer access to the tunic worn underneath, two vertical slits are cut on the chest and covered with a flap. The skirt and cuffs are gathered by elasticized bands. The sleeve-ends are made of the same material as the smock but in colors more subdued. The 'autumn' side of the smock shows its tan and brown pattern through the chest opening. Two overstitched holes are provided on the back and on the chest. This smock has all the characteristics of the early types.

The man wears a camouflage field cap. His helmet is hooked to the belt. Both the cap and helmet cover are cut in the same camouflage material which features a sharply defined, light, medium and dark green pattern on a beige background.
The 'Tarnjacke' (camouflage smock) is worn over the tunic. Fitted with elasticized bands, the cuffs and the skirt are tucked up for comfort.

The standard issue weapon is a K-98k rifle.

The tapered trousers are made of field gray cloth. The legs are gathered in canvas anklets fitted with two leather buckle straps.
The mountain boots are made of black leather and secure with seven pairs of eyelets.

105

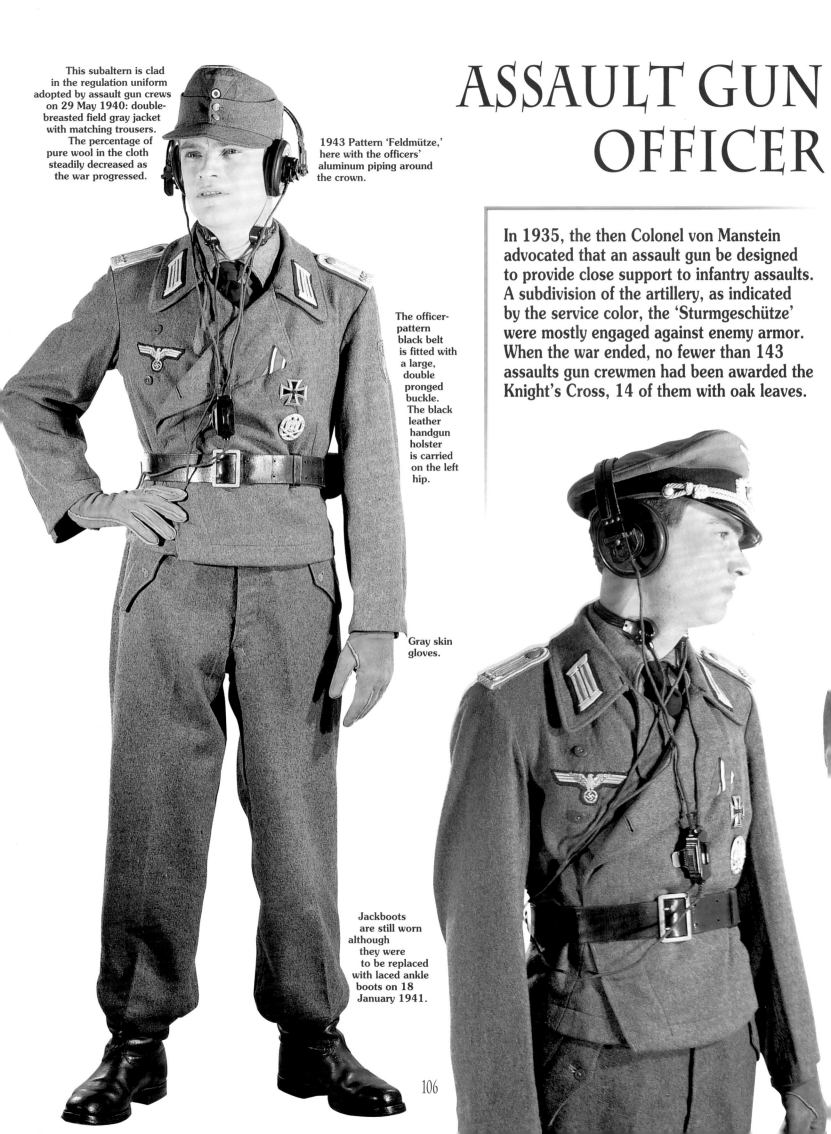

ASSAULT GUN OFFICER

This subaltern is clad in the regulation uniform adopted by assault gun crews on 29 May 1940: double-breasted field gray jacket with matching trousers. The percentage of pure wool in the cloth steadily decreased as the war progressed.

1943 Pattern 'Feldmütze,' here with the officers' aluminum piping around the crown.

The officer-pattern black belt is fitted with a large, double pronged buckle. The black leather handgun holster is carried on the left hip.

In 1935, the then Colonel von Manstein advocated that an assault gun be designed to provide close support to infantry assaults. A subdivision of the artillery, as indicated by the service color, the 'Sturmgeschütze' were mostly engaged against enemy armor. When the war ended, no fewer than 143 assaults gun crewmen had been awarded the Knight's Cross, 14 of them with oak leaves.

Gray skin gloves.

Jackboots are still worn although they were to be replaced with laced ankle boots on 18 January 1941.

The trousers for assault gun crews were fastened around the waist with a hemmed-in belt fitted with a three-pronged steel buckle. The pockets have button flaps (except the fob pocket which is fitted with a metal ring). The six buttons of the 1944 Pattern trousers are made of pressed cardboard. Securing with drawstrings, the bottom of the trouser legs have slits buttoning at ankle level for a closer fit.

Left.
The jacket closes down the front with seven buttons. The seventh one is sewn at collar level. The label stitched to the gray sateen lining indicates that the garment was made in 1943 by a Hamburg manufacturer. The two inner pockets are also made of green sateen. The cuffs can be gathered with a button and the collar secures with a metal hook.

The 1935 Pattern peaked cap is piped in bright red like the shoulder straps and collar tabs. The artilleryman has been awarded four decorations: the ribbons of the Iron Cross 2nd Class and 1941-42 Eastern Campaign medals are stitched through a buttonhole, and the Iron Cross 1st Class is pinned to the chest above the General combat badge. The 'Kuban' shield commemorating the 1943 siege is worn on the left sleeve.

Below.
Throat microphone and headset, P-38 handgun in its 1944 Pattern holster and ordnance map: such were the indispensable tools of the officer in the field. The officer's 1938 Pattern sidecap (piped in silver cord around the turn-up and crown) retains the red arm-of-service 'soutache' which was officially dropped on 8 September 1942.

1944. This second-lieutenant is commissioned with the 66th Assault Gun Group as shown by the gilt metal figures on his shoulder straps. The backing of the straps and the piping of the collar patches is in bright red. A knit gray shirt and a black tie are worn under the double-breasted jacket.

'GROSSDEUTSCHLAND' INFANTRY OFFICER

The Close combat clasp in gold ('Nahkampfspange') is secured above the left chest pocket, above the Iron Cross 1st Class, the Infantry combat badge and the Silver wound badge (awarded for three or four wounds). The Iron Cross 2nd Class ribbon is slipped through the second buttonhole down the front. The tunic's metal buttons are finished in field gray.

The black leather officer's belt is fitted with a pronged buckle. The P-38 holster is carried on the left hip.

The breeches are cut in the same quality cloth as the cap and the tunic but look slightly greener. The black leather riding boots are polished to a shiny finish.

Right.
The 'Schirmmütze' cap is made of regulation field-gray cloth. The crown and the dark bluish-green band are piped in white, the service color of the 'Panzer Korps Füsilier Regiment' of the 'Großdeutschland' Panzer Corps. The peak is made of black-lacquered vulcanised fiber. The national emblem, cockade and eagle are woven in aluminum thread on a dark bluish-green backing. The cap has neither cords nor buttons.

The tunic is cut in the same thick field gray cloth as the cap. The box pleated pockets have three-pointed button flaps. The sleeves have turned-back cuffs. The shoulder straps are made of white cloth adorned with double 'U'-shaped aluminum braiding. The star rank badge is made of embossed metal. The 'GD' (Großdeutschland) ciphers, whose gold wash has worn off, are pinned on. The dark blue-green collar tabs bear aluminum 'tresse' braid enhanced by a stripe of white silk down the middle. On the chest, the eagle is woven in silver bullion on a dark bluish-green underlay. As per regulations, the unit cuff title is stitched to the right sleeve one centimeter above the sleeve end.

On 1 December 1944, Helmut H. was awarded the Gold Close combat clasp, the highest decoration which could be bestowed on a German infantryman.

It was awarded for fighting for 50 days in hand-to hand engagements where individual weapons and cold steel often made the decision. Now aged 34, the second-lieutenant is commissioned with the HQ Company of the 'Großdeutschland' Panzer Corps 'Füsilier' Regiment (infantry). Exceptionally, H. has been granted a 21 days' furlough and, after being promoted to a higher rank, is about to rejoin his unit based in Prussia near Willenberg.

The officer sidecap is cut in the same cloth as all the other field gray garments worn by the officer. It has a gray on green woven eagle the cockade being hand-embroidered.

Designed by Wilhelm Ernest Peekhaus of Berlin, the Gold Close Combat Clasp is cast in fine gilt zinc. The clasp measures 98 mm by 26 mm taken at the widest point. The gold clasp was usually better crafted than the two lower grades.

Above.

'Großdeutschland' cuff title, fourth type, introduced in October 1944. The silver gray thread lettering in gothic long hand is embroidered on a black sateen cloth tape piped in silver gray near the edges.

The officer has donned his rubberized coat. Made of gray material, this double-breasted garment has two rows of six buttons down the front. The collar is secured with two hooks. The slanted side pockets are covered with wide flaps. The only insignia are the shoulder straps secured by a loop near the armhole seam and buttoned near the collar. The 'GD' ciphers have retained some of their original gold finish. The metal buttons are finished in field gray.

MOUNTAIN ENGINEER OFFICER

The ribbon bar of the Iron Cross 2nd Class, the 1941-42 Russian Campaign Medal and the decoration awarded for four years' service with the Wehrmacht is stitched to the tunic (the latter has a small silver eagle which may also indicate up the 18 years' service).
The breeches are made of fine gray cloth.
The legs adjust with zips down the ankles.
The high boots are made of black leather.

Positioned with his men on the Gustav Line (italian front) in late January 1944, this 5th Mountain Engineer Division officer will hardly ever have the opportunity to wear his service dress and so proudly to display the 'Kreta' cuff title he was awarded for his part in the invasion of Crete. He was still a junior NCO when on 25 May 1941, he captured the city of Kastelli with the 95th Mountain Engineer Battalion.

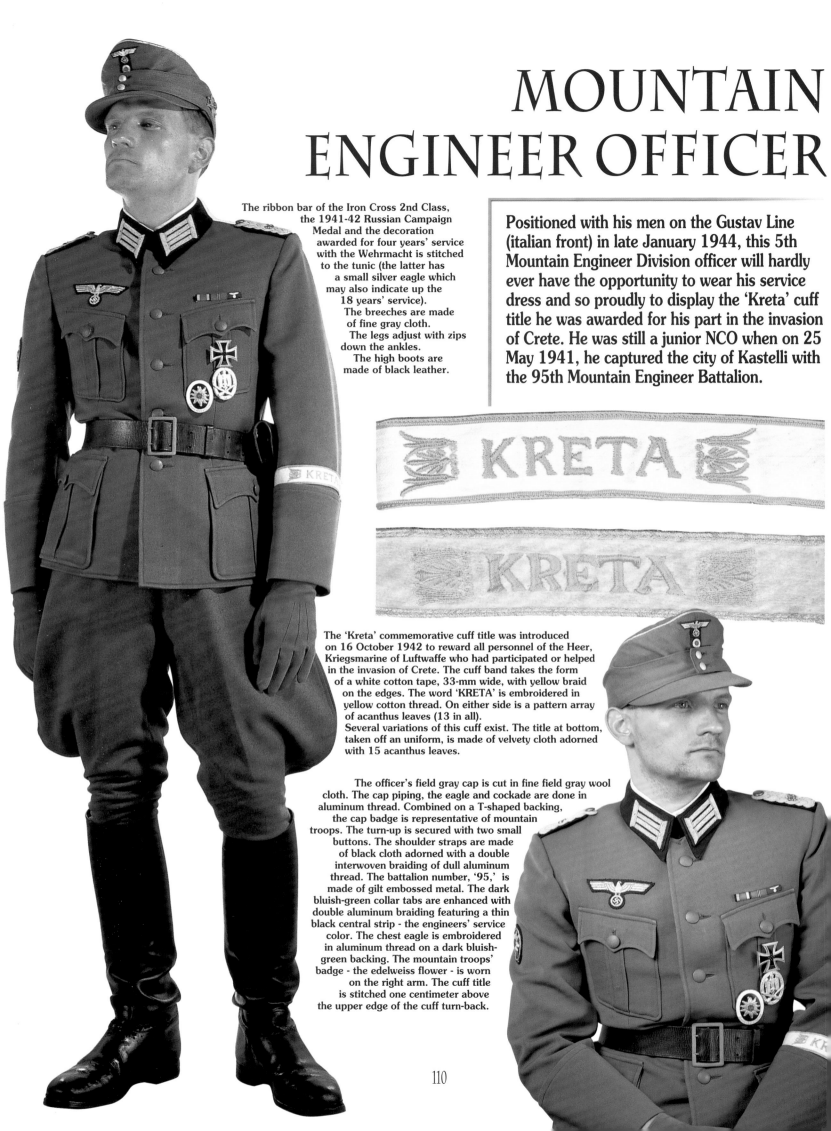

The 'Kreta' commemorative cuff title was introduced on 16 October 1942 to reward all personnel of the Heer, Kriegsmarine of Luftwaffe who had participated or helped in the invasion of Crete. The cuff band takes the form of a white cotton tape, 33-mm wide, with yellow braid on the edges. The word 'KRETA' is embroidered in yellow cotton thread. On either side is a pattern array of acanthus leaves (13 in all).
Several variations of this cuff exist. The title at bottom, taken off an uniform, is made of velvety cloth adorned with 15 acanthus leaves.

The officer's field gray cap is cut in fine field gray wool cloth. The cap piping, the eagle and cockade are done in aluminum thread. Combined on a T-shaped backing, the cap badge is representative of mountain troops. The turn-up is secured with two small buttons. The shoulder straps are made of black cloth adorned with a double interwoven braiding of dull aluminum thread. The battalion number, '95,' is made of gilt embossed metal. The dark bluish-green collar tabs are enhanced with double aluminum braiding featuring a thin black central strip - the engineers' service color. The chest eagle is embroidered in aluminum thread on a dark bluish-green backing. The mountain troops' badge - the edelweiss flower - is worn on the right arm. The cuff title is stitched one centimeter above the upper edge of the cuff turn-back.

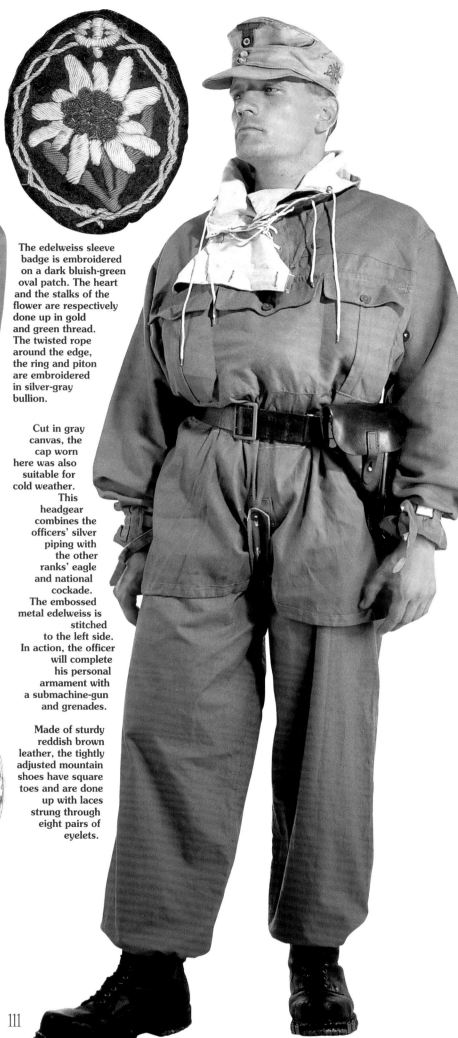

The edelweiss sleeve badge is embroidered on a dark bluish-green oval patch. The heart and the stalks of the flower are respectively done up in gold and green thread. The twisted rope around the edge, the ring and piton are embroidered in silver-gray bullion.

Cut in gray canvas, the cap worn here was also suitable for cold weather. This headgear combines the officers' silver piping with the other ranks' eagle and national cockade. The embossed metal edelweiss is stitched to the left side. In action, the officer will complete his personal armament with a submachine-gun and grenades.

Made of sturdy reddish brown leather, the tightly adjusted mountain shoes have square toes and are done up with laces strung through eight pairs of eyelets.

Above and right.
The reversible windproof smock has an integral hood and three patch pockets on the chest. These are sewn side by side and covered by a buttoned flap each. The left and right pockets feature a central pleat. The garment is gathered at the waist by a sliding tape, and by straps at the wrists, secured by metal buckles. A wide tab passes between the legs to prevent the smock from riding up the chest.
The canvas overpants are held at the waist by a-hemmed-in cloth belt. All buttons are pressed paper.
The leg bottoms are tightened thanks to sliding tapes.

The Iron Cross 1st Class (top) is pinned to the left pocket. Exceptionally, this medal is finished in black enamel.
The General Combat Badge (right) is finished in dull silver (originally intended as the Engineers Combat Badge but redesigned in June 1940 to include other services). The Heer Mountain Guide (left) badge also has a dull silver finish and features a metal edelweiss set on a dark green enameled oval, edged in gold.
Established in the 1930s, this badge was already awarded within the pre-war Reichswehr.

'GROSSDEUTSCHLAND' RECCE COMPANY NCO

The 1943 1943 Pattern 'Feldmütze' sports the imperial eagle in gray thread, and the national cockade, both woven on a black backing. The turn-up is kept up with two black buttons. The lining is made of green sateen. Cut in black wool cloth, the short double-breasted jacket is worn over a gray shirt and black tie. It fastens on the side to seven button and at waist level with a drawstring. The cuff slits have a double button arrangement. In this picture, the chest eagle is concealed under the right lapel. The unit cuff title is stitched to the bottom of the right sleeve. The shoulder straps are secured with a loop at the armhole seam and buttoned near the collar. The collar tabs are piped in golden yellow - the service color of recce units - and adorned with an embossed metal death's head.

The Iron Cross 1st Class and the Tank combat badge 2nd Class ('Panzerkampf-abzeichen') are pinned to the left side of the chest. The P-08 pistol black leather holster is fastened to the left side. The black leather belt is fitted with a late type belt buckle finished in flat dark gray.

Made of matching black cloth, the regulation trousers are fastened with a hemmed-in belt, securing with a metal pronged buckle. The tapered legs are gathered around the ankle with a button and lacing arrangement.

The ankle boots are made of black leather.

October 1944. Elements of the 'Großdeutschland' Panzer Grenadier Division were positioned between Tryskaja and Plunge to the east of Memel in eastern Prussia.

Heavily outnumbered, the Germans defenders eventually yielded to the overwhelming pressure of Russian armor. However soon after, the group's 'Jagdpanzer' 38t Hetzer and the 'Schützenpanzerwagen' (half-tracks) intervened and checked the outflanking move. This study depicts a sergeant of the divisional 'Panzeraufklärungsabteilung' (reconnaissance battalion) as he is retreating with his unit.

The sergeant's shoulder straps are made of black cloth and piped in yellow; they bear the NCO silver braiding as well as the divisional 'GD' (Großdeutschland) gothic cipher, woven in golden yellow thread. The arm-of-service color of reconnaissance units changed many times: originally pink, it was replaced with golden yellow in 1938. In 1939, golden brown was intended to be used but this color was instead attributed to motorcyclist battalions. Finally, the service color of 'Auflärungsabteilung' reverted to pink in 1941 but how strictly enforced the final directive was - particularly among front line units - is difficult to ascertain.

The suit and cap have been locally-made from tent section material, in the classic 'splinter' pattern. The shade of the cap is darker than that of the jacket while the trousers are lighter. The trousers have been tailored by a skilled craftsman, whereas the cap and the jacket have unmistakably been manufactured in a larger shop. The 1943 Pattern field cap has a green lining and a stitched-on simulated turn-up.

Above.
The jacket has five field gray painted buttons down the front. The waist is fastened with a large strap buttoning over to the right. The straight edged pocket flaps have one button each. The gray lining is provided with an inner pocket. The shoulder straps are secured with a loop over the armhole seam and a button near the collar.

Right.
Instituted on 2 July 1943, the '25' Class Tank combat badge was awarded for taking part in 25 tank engagements on different days, or for 15 months' uninterrupted service on the front lines. The badge could also be awarded for a serious wound. The number of points required to obtain the award was recorded by the company commander. The original badge was instituted on 20 July 1939 and awarded for taking part in three tank engagements on three different days. Initially known as 'Panzerkampfwagenabzeichen' (tank badge) it was renamed 'Panzerkampfabzeichen' (tank combat badge) on 1 June 1940. Initially meant for armored crews, its award was extended in 1942 to the motorcyclists of armored divisions and to the recovery teams who often had to perform their tasks on the front line. The awarding criteria were the same as for tank crews. Designed by Ernest Peekhaus, the badge consists of an oval wreath of gilt oak leaves and acorns. On the apex is an eagle clutching a swastika in its talons. A dark gray tank passes through the wreath from left to right. The tablet with the raised numeral '25' is finished in brass on a black finished recess (the black paint has worn off here). The wreath and eagle are finished in dull silver.

The loose fitting trousers are gathered around the waist by a belt slipped through loops of matching material. The buttons used for the fly (four) and the thigh pocket flaps (one each) are the dished metal models used on shelter halves. The leg bottoms are secured with drawstrings.

Previous page.
The division's name is embroidered in gothic long hand on a black wool cloth tape. Silver gray thread was used for both the lettering and the piping near the edges.

The warm reversible parka is padded with wool off-cuts (except the hood). The camouflage pattern consists of dark green and brown blotches on a pale green background. The blotches have both blurred and sharp edges. For improved camouflage effect, a pattern of thin green lines has been randomly applied over the field gray backing. The garment is done up with six metal buttons fitting into double buttonholes. The skirt pockets have slanted button flaps. The bottom of the skirt and the hood are gathered with a drawstring. The waist is tightened with a hemmed-in belt. The cuffs have buttons for the same purpose.

GRENADIER, COURLAND

'Here they come!' The soldiers of 'Heeresgruppe Kurland' (Kurland Army Corps) trapped between the Baltic Sea and the Gulf of Riga braced themselves when the front-line erupted into flames. The Soviets rushed the German positions and soon, after fierce fighting, eight of their divisions had broken through.

Deployed to the south of Libau, the 126th Infantry Division was in the thick of the fighting but soon managed to plug the gap and established a strong defensive line.

The ammunition pouches for the K-98k rifle and a stick grenade are carried on the black leather belt fitted with a dark green buckle. An egg-shaped hand grenade is dangling from one of the ammunition pouches. The field gray trousers are tucked into leather jackboots.

The commemorative 'Kurland' cuff title was instituted on a request from General Oberst von Wietinghoff, who commanded 'Courland' Army Group, a force comprizing the 16th and 18th Armies which totaled 18 divisions. On 12 March 1945, the OKW (German High Command) ordered that the cuff title be issued to the defenders of the besieged region of Latvia. The cuff title was produced locally at a Kuldiga weaving mill and awarded to soldiers who had taken part in three engagements or sustained a wound while in the sector (soldiers of ancillary units who had served for three months with 'Heeresgruppe Kurland' were also eligible for the title). The cuff title is made of grayish white tape of variable width (35 to 37 mm, for the examples shown here). Also showing marked differences are the lettering and the size of the devices on either side of the inscription. These are the crest of the Grand Master of the Teutonic Knights and the moose head borrowed from the emblem of Mitau). The title was either woven (top model) or embroidered (two bottom models) in black thread. The same applies to the white piping along the edges. These differences result from the small quantities procured from local craftsmen (some have even been printed).

Initially painted field gray, the helmet has been daubed with a loose pattern of irregular green patches over a sand background. The paint was liberally mixed with dirt for a grainy, non reflective flat finish.

The 1943-Pattern field cap is in field gray cloth. The turn-up is fastened with two gray metal buttons. The eagle and the cockade are woven on a common trapezoidal rayon patch.

The tunic and cap are cut in the same woolen material. The shoulder straps are piped in white, the 'grenadier' (infantry) branch color. The ¾collar 'Litzen' are woven in two different shades of gray thread. Stitched above the right chest pocket, the eagle is woven in gray thread on a pale green underlay. The corporal rank chevron is displayed on the left sleeve. The tunic has six buttons down the front and box-pleated pockets with pointed button flap. The skirt pockets feature a side bellows for expansion. The cuff slits are fastened with two synthetic buttons. The other buttons are field gray finished¾metal.

The cuff title is stitched in 14.5 cm above the left sleeve edge. A ribbon bar for the following awards is visible above the left chest pocket: the Iron Cross 2nd Class, the (Kriegsverdienst Kreuz (War Merit Medal) and the 1941-42 Russian Winter Campaign medal. Pinned above the ribbons, the Bronze class close combat clasp, a highly distinguished order, was awarded for 15 days close combat.

The Iron Cross 1st Class and the Infantry Combat Badge are pinned onto the left breast pocket.

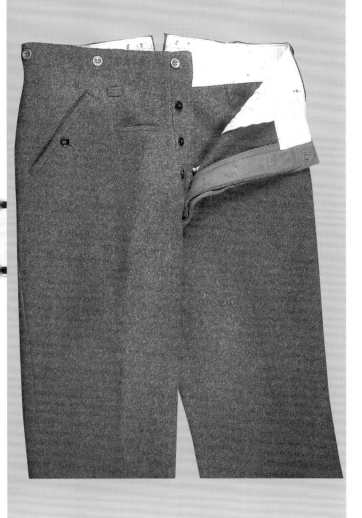

The straight trousers are cut in field gray cloth (showing a slightly brownish hue). They are lined with white cotton cloth around the waist; the same material is used for the side and hip pockets. The hip pockets have one button each and the fob pocket has neither flap nor button. The four fly buttons are made of black synthetic material whereas those used for fastening the braces are made of metal (dished type). The fly reinforcement is made of gray cloth. The half belt on the small of the back tighten with a double-pronged buckle.

'LIST' INFANTRY REGIMENT OFFICER

The officer is wearing the going-out uniform. The ¾high-quality Schirmmütze has aluminum bullion insignia. The tricolor cockade is prominent.

The aluminum cord is retained by two small buttons. Both tunic and breeches are cut from high quality Italian cloth for officer uniforms.

The tunic is fastened with six buttons. The pleated pockets close with three-pointed button flaps. The sleeves have straight.

The bluish dark-green collar with two metal hooks sports late-war collar tabs, in dull gray thread and braided white arm-of-service piping. The shoulder straps are sewn at the shoulder and held near the collar by screw-on buttons.

The national emblem is embroidered with aluminum thread onto blue-green facing material.

The ribbons of the Iron Cross Second Class, the Eastern Front Winter 1941 Medal and the Four Years' Army Service Medal (struck with a silver eagle) have been pinned above the left pocket.
The Iron Cross, First Class and the Infantry Combat badge are pinned to the left pocket. The 'Krimschild' - the Crimea shield - has been sewn on the left sleeve. The cuff title of the 199th Regiment has been sewn above the turn-back cuffs.

The brown leather belt is a captured Russian item. It supports a holster containing a 7.65-mm automatic pistol. Our officer here has chosen to wear (in a breach of orders) a pair of mounted officer's riding breeches, with gray leather reinforcement inside the thighs, tucked into black leather boots.

The gloves are made of gray chamois leather without press studs.

At the end of September 1939, the 199th Infantry Regiment, one of the three infantry regiments of the 57th Division, recently created in Wehrkreis VII (XXXX) became the upholder of the traditions of the List Regiment, the 16th Bavarian Infantry Reserve Regiment whose commander, Colonel List, was killed during the Great War.

After spending several months in Normandy, the 57th Infantry Division was permanently committed on the Eastern Front, particularly in the Kharkov sector at the end of 1941, and once again in the summer of 1943. At the beginning of 1944 the 57th was at Tcherkassy. It was in Belorussia, at Mogilev on the Dniepr, in May and June 1944 that the 199th all but ceased to exist in the fighting. The traditions of the old 16th Bavarian were kept up by the 19th Grenadier Regiment (7th Infantry Division) on 31 August 1944.

Above and opposite page.
1934-model Feldmütze. This light and soft field cap is made of fine feldgrau wool. The pliable visor is made of black varnished leather without binding on the edge. The national emblem, cockade and oak leaves are woven with aluminum thread on an olive green background. The dark bluish green facing cloth band was added in ¾1935. The cap is piped in white on the crown and band, for the infantry.

The Krimschild ('Crimea' armshield) was instituted by Adolf Hitler on 25 July 1942 and awarded to soldiers in the following circumstances. They had to have:
- Taken part in the fighting in the Crimea between 21 September 1941 and 4 July 1942
- Been present in the sector for at least three months
- Been wounded or taken part in a major engagement
The award document had to be signed by Feldmarschall Erich von Manstein, commanding XI Army. The decoration shown here has been made slightly bronzed zinc plate, slightly curved. The ¾ backing patch is in feldgrau cloth.

The unlined summer tunic has been made out of strong light gray wool and linen cloth. It closes down the front by means of six metal buttons.
The box-pleated chest pockets are shut by pointed button flaps.
The shoulder straps, for an infantry lieutenant, are of flat aluminum braid on a white facing cloth backing.
On a dark blue-green oblong background, the collar tabs are embroidered in silver wire, with white median stripes.
The eagle is woven with gray thread on a dark blue-green background.
The 6 x 30 sand painted binoculars have their rubber lens cap and a tab to hold them to a tunic button.
Two 1924-model stick grenades and the green canvas pouch (left side) for MP40 magazines have been slipped onto the black leather officer belt.
The pistol holster cannot be seen here.

The breeches are cut in tough Feldgrau-colored cloth.
The high boots are the officer's pattern.

A

B

The unit cuff title band was issued to regimental personnel from December 1943, from January 1944 for the reserve battalion and from September 1944 for the 19th Grenadier-Regiment.
Fig. A band shows signs of wear. The inscription is done in light gray, now yellowed, thread on a base of dark green bluish satin wool, bordered with aluminum wire piping. Fig. B band shows a longer inscription; it is fine and straight and the thread has kept its original color, embroidered on dark green woolen cloth and edged with gray thread piping.

The armored crews double breasted jacket is tailored in fine black wool gaberdine. The high quality finish was obtained by a tailor in Florence and duly bears his label.

The jacket is fly-fronted on the right side with four black buttons. The shoulder flaps are made of pink facing cloth superimposed with aluminum braiding and a golden metal star.

The airforce-pattern chest eagle is embroidered in silver thread. The cuff title is stitched 5 inches from the bottom of the right sleeve. The ribbons of the Iron Cross, Second Class, War Merit cross with swords and Sudeten Commemorative Medal are worn on the right chest. The Iron Cross, First Class, Luftwaffe Ground Combat badge and Silver wound badge are pinned above the belt on the left side.

The black trousers are the special issue to Army tank and armored car crews.

The gloves are made of dark gray chamois leather.

The boots are made of dark brown leather.

On 14 July 1944, the «Hermann Göring» Fallschirmpanzerdivision was still in the Florence sector. The retreating German army took part in violent counter-attacks. Indeed, on 3 June, faced with the pressure from the Allies, Marshall Kettering declared Rome an open city and undertook what turned out to be a masterly strategic retreat.

The airforce officer 'Schirmmütze' has a rigid fiber visor with a black lacquer finish. The edge is bound with black waxed cloth. The cord is held on the sides by a small button painted matt silver. The silver embroidered wings and oak leaf wreath design on the band surrounds a tricolor cockade. The top is made of gray-blue wool gaberdine. All the piping and the silver embroidery are made of aluminum wire. The gray cotton shirt is worn with a black tie. The short jacket's collar is edged in silver cord. The white collar tabs are in the distinctive color of the Hermann Göring division, with the armored troops' death's heads in pressed white metal.

Although wearing the walking-out dress, the lieutenant is wearing the later Fliegermütze made of gray-blue woolen cloth. The turn-up is held at the front by a single dark gray metal button. The insignia are the other ranks' pattern: eagle in dull gray and tricolor. Only the aluminum cord on the top reveals that this is an officer's hat.

The open-neck tunic is made from fine gray-blue wool gaberdine, closed by four metal buttons. The four box-pleated pockets close with button flaps.

The eagle on the chest is embroidered in silver on a gray background which overlaps onto the pocket flap. The ribbon of the Iron Cross, Second Class is slipped through the first buttonhole.

Above.
Detail of the 'Hermann Göring' Division insignia. The shoulder straps of the gray-blue going-out uniform are piped in white, the divisional color, whereas those of the black field uniform are edged in pink (the branch color). The collar tabs respectively bear rank insignia for a lieutenant, and the traditional 'Totenkopf' of armored formations, in pressed white metal.

Below.
The cuff title is a late-war manufacture for officers. The tape backing is blue, with aluminum wire embroidered letters and silver wire piping on the edges. The title is affixed 5 inches from the sleeve end.

HERMANN GÖRING

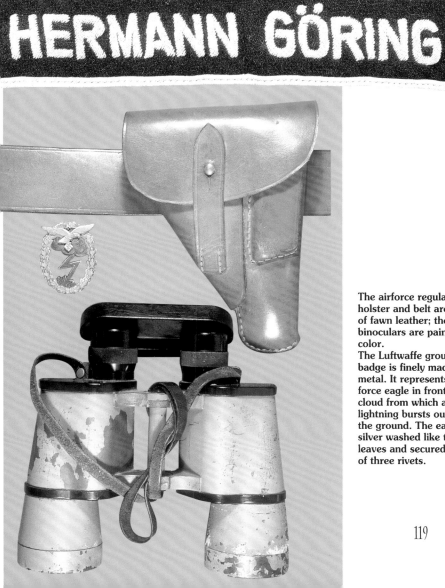

The airforce regulation pistol holster and belt are made of fawn leather; the 7 x 50 binoculars are painted sand color.
The Luftwaffe ground combat badge is finely made in metal. It represents the air force eagle in front of a gray cloud from which a streak of lightning bursts out to strike the ground. The eagle is dull silver washed like the oak leaves and secured by means of three rivets.

1945

(© Bundesarchiv)

SCHUTZPOLIZEI ON THE EASTERN FRONT

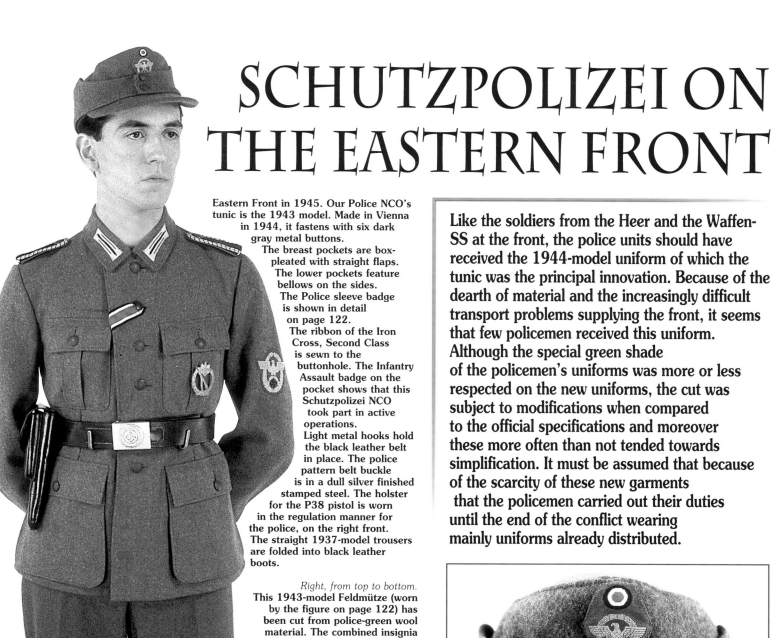

Eastern Front in 1945. Our Police NCO's tunic is the 1943 model. Made in Vienna in 1944, it fastens with six dark gray metal buttons.

The breast pockets are box-pleated with straight flaps. The lower pockets feature bellows on the sides.

The Police sleeve badge is shown in detail on page 122.

The ribbon of the Iron Cross, Second Class is sewn to the buttonhole. The Infantry Assault badge on the pocket shows that this Schutzpolizei NCO took part in active operations.

Light metal hooks hold the black leather belt in place. The police pattern belt buckle is in a dull silver finished stamped steel. The holster for the P38 pistol is worn in the regulation manner for the police, on the right front. The straight 1937-model trousers are folded into black leather boots.

Right, from top to bottom.
This 1943-model Feldmütze (worn by the figure on page 122) has been cut from police-green wool material. The combined insignia shows the ¾ cockade and the police eagle embroidered in gray thread, on a pale green background.

This other 1943 Feldmütze has a rather more classic cut, with a taller top. The insignia is the same as the forage cap on page 123. This quality headdress was made in 1944.

Like the soldiers from the Heer and the Waffen-SS at the front, the police units should have received the 1944-model uniform of which the tunic was the principal innovation. Because of the dearth of material and the increasingly difficult transport problems supplying the front, it seems that few policemen received this uniform. Although the special green shade of the policemen's uniforms was more or less respected on the new uniforms, the cut was subject to modifications when compared to the official specifications and moreover these more often than not tended towards simplification. It must be assumed that because of the scarcity of these new garments that the policemen carried out their duties until the end of the conflict wearing mainly uniforms already distributed.

The police arm badge for the field uniform is woven from gray thread on a green background.

Our man seen has now been issued with the new 1944-pattern short jacket. This has been cut from indifferent quality Police green material in a Viennese workshop in 1945. The garment closes down the front thanks to six metal buttons, including two on the waistband. A buttoned tab under the collar can hold the collar up. The patch pocket flaps have buttons. A vent in the cuff seam allows the sleeves to be rolled up. The black Wound badge has been added to the two preceding decorations.

Below.
1944-pattern short jacket in police green cloth. This variation is well finished but the pointed pocket flaps without buttons, the absence of the vent at the cuff, the narrow strip at the waist with one button, the fastening reduced to five buttons on the front, the absence of inside pockets and lining are differences when compared with the issue model shown on the figure at right.

The bottom of the trousers are tightened and held by green canvas gaiters. The boots are made of black leather.

The police side cap insignia is woven in white thread on a black background. The curtain is piped in light green. The shirt is made from green cotton and fastened by four buttons.

Right.
The 1942-type steel helmet bears the Police shield decal. The uniform is suited to the warm season. The police green drill tunic is cut on the same pattern as the 1943-model issue wool garment. It is not lined however, and its buttons are detachable.

The rifle clip carriers have been slipped onto the black leather belt. The bread bag, water bottle, mess tin, and the bayonet in its leather frog are placed in the small of the back and they cannot be seen here.

1. These field trousers (made in 1943) are cut from thick wool material. Synthetic buttons on the waistband hold the braces. The pocket openings are slanted. A hip pocket has been inserted on the right. There is a half-belt on the back.
2. 1943 model (made in 1944) Police field trousers: the legs are tapered. The brace buttons are placed on the inside of the waistband. The front pockets are buttoned. The fob pocket is covered with a buttoned flap.
A tab and buckle

have been fitted to the waist on each side. Buttoned belt loops on the front and back are used to hold the leather belt. The buttocks are reinforced by a large patch. The hip pocket is on the right. All the buttons are synthetic and painted dark green. The lining and the pockets are cut from light brown sateen and green cloth.
3. The straight drill trousers have a patch fob pocket. The pocket slits are vertical and the trousers do not have a half-belt in the back. Braces can be worn.

ARMY SHARPSHOOTER

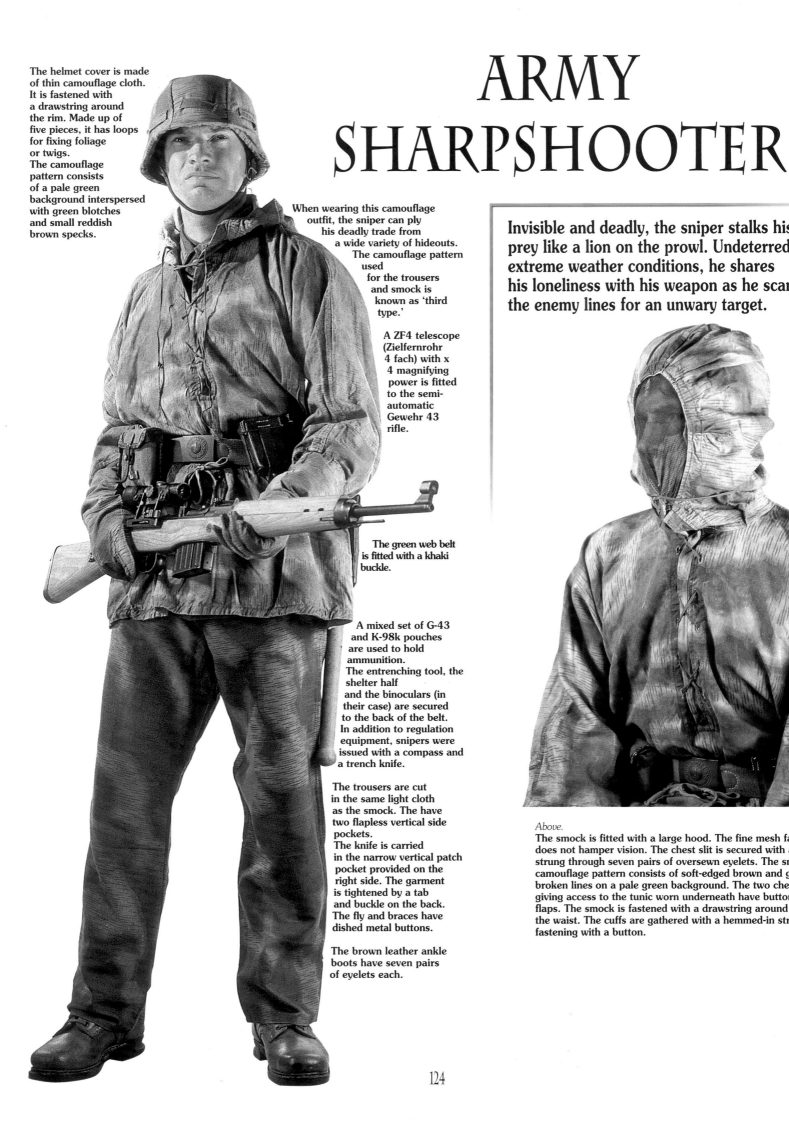

The helmet cover is made of thin camouflage cloth. It is fastened with a drawstring around the rim. Made up of five pieces, it has loops for fixing foliage or twigs. The camouflage pattern consists of a pale green background interspersed with green blotches and small reddish brown specks.

When wearing this camouflage outfit, the sniper can ply his deadly trade from a wide variety of hideouts. The camouflage pattern used for the trousers and smock is known as 'third type.'

A ZF4 telescope (Zielfernrohr 4 fach) with x 4 magnifying power is fitted to the semi-automatic Gewehr 43 rifle.

The green web belt is fitted with a khaki buckle.

A mixed set of G-43 and K-98k pouches are used to hold ammunition. The entrenching tool, the shelter half and the binoculars (in their case) are secured to the back of the belt. In addition to regulation equipment, snipers were issued with a compass and a trench knife.

The trousers are cut in the same light cloth as the smock. The have two flapless vertical side pockets. The knife is carried in the narrow vertical patch pocket provided on the right side. The garment is tightened by a tab and buckle on the back. The fly and braces have dished metal buttons.

The brown leather ankle boots have seven pairs of eyelets each.

Invisible and deadly, the sniper stalks his prey like a lion on the prowl. Undeterred by extreme weather conditions, he shares his loneliness with his weapon as he scans the enemy lines for an unwary target.

Above.
The smock is fitted with a large hood. The fine mesh face veil does not hamper vision. The chest slit is secured with a lace strung through seven pairs of oversewn eyelets. The smock's camouflage pattern consists of soft-edged brown and green broken lines on a pale green background. The two chest slits giving access to the tunic worn underneath have buttonless flaps. The smock is fastened with a drawstring around the waist. The cuffs are gathered with a hemmed-in strap fastening with a button.

The white oversuit was used for sniping in snowbound environments. Its hood is tied around the neck with tapes. The smock is made of off-white cotton material and closes with four buttons down the front. The large box pleated chest pockets have pointed flaps. The cuffs are fastened with buttoned straps. The trousers are loose fitting so they can be worn over thick, warmer clothing. The fly, the ankle tabs and the thigh pockets are fastened with buttons made of white pressed cardboard.

The 'Zeltbahn' tent section is made of water repellent cotton. It is secured with two black leather straps when rolled up for carrying on the pack. The mittens are cut in the same non-reversible thin cloth as the helmet cover. The magazine pouches for the G-43 rifle are manufactured from sturdy gray-green canvas reinforced with leather strips along the edges. Each pouch holds a single clip.

The 1943 Pattern 'Feldmütze' is made of field gray cloth. The turn-up is fastened with two pebbled metal buttons. The death's head on the front and the eagle on the left side are woven in gray thread on a black background. For extra protection against the cold, the soldier has donned a tube-like, stretchable gray wool balaclava under the cap.

The sheepskin three-quarter length coat affords superlative protection in wintry conditions. The garment is lined with wool (brown for the coat and sleeves and less conspicuous

white for the collar). The coat has two flapless side pockets and closes with four leather buttons.

The black leather belt is fitted with a painted buckle. The P-38 handgun and the tool kit were on regular issue to machine-gun crews. The gloves are made of gray wool. The reversible trousers are padded with wool off-cuts. They are fastened with a drawstring at the waist. The trouser legs are tucked into the black leather boots.

'TOTENFOPF' MACHINE-GUNNER

The weather was bitterly cold when the 3rd 'Totenkopf' SS Panzer Division led by Brigadeführer (brigadier) Helmut Becker tried to relieve Budapest. Lasting from 1 to 13 January 1945, the operation only forestalled the inevitable end.

This machine-gunner took part in the action alongside his comrades of the divisional armored recce group.

REGULATION ACCESSORIES ISSUED TO MACHINE-GUN TEAMS.
1. Bolt cleaning fluid.
2. Oil can (shaped so two can fit in an ammunition box).
3. Spares box (holding various parts for the breech etc.).
4. Saddle drum carrier (each drum holds 50 rounds).
5. 1941 Pattern ammunition box (holding 300 7.92¾mm rounds).
6. Carrying strap ('Tragegurt') suitable for ammunition, weapons, etc.
7. Spare bolt spring in its box.
8. Flash hider and bolt cover

REGULATION ITEMS FOR MACHINE-GUN TEAM NUMBER 1 (GUNNER):
9. Stamped metal anti-aircraft sight.
10. Oiler.
11. Case extractor (damaged case rim).
12. Spare bolt.
13. Ammunition belt feeding tab.
14. Blank firing adaptor.
15. Machine gunner's pouch (leather pattern).
16. Asbestos gloves for quick barrel change.
17. Extractor disassembly tool.
18. Case extractor (undamaged case rim).
19. Breech extractor and firing pin pouch.

The MG-42 was manufactured in 1943 by Gustloff Werke (factory code 'dfb'). This updated weapon was fitted with an MG-34 bipod and had a folding vertical cocking lever as one of its most distinctive features.

The helmet cover is made of two types of cloth: the panel stretching from the visor over the top of the head to the nape carries a figure '4' and presents a green and dark green pattern on a beige background. The side panels carry a figure '6' and display a greenish pattern with dark green mottling over wide, dark brown blotches. The corporal stands in his 1943-45 Pattern field gray tunic sealing with five matching buttons down the front. The ¾ pocket flaps have straight edges. The collar secures with a hook.

Below.
1943 Pattern 'Totenkopf' cuff title. Manufactured by BeVo of Wuppertal, the title is woven with black and white artificial silk. It was stitched 14.5 cm above the edge of the cuff.

The regulation MG team No 1 (gunner) large leather pouch and assault pack are fastened to the black leather belt and suspension straps. Asbestos gloves and an egg-shaped grenade are secured to the ¾ pouch.

Totenkopf

4

15

16

12

9

10

14

13

18

17

19

11

The helmet cover is made of cotton and shows a camouflage scheme of sharply defined, rounded, irregular patches on a golden brown and tan background.

A tube-like balaclava helmet is rolled up around the neck and covers the collar of the gray jersey shirt.

BELGIAN VOLUNTEER, POMERANIA

Deployed on the Pomeranian front I February 1945, the 'Wallonie' 28th SS Division had dwindled to a 2,000 man 'Kampfgruppe' in the final months of the Eastern front struggle.

Made up of Belgian volunteers, the unit was positioned to the south of Stargard in a last attempt to stem the Soviet offensive which was sweeping from the Vistula to the Oder. Through the rain and cold, the 'Bourguignons' fought their last battle and held their ground to the last man

Left.
Woven on field gray patch, the Belgian volunteers' arm shield presented the Belgian national colors of black, yellow and red. Although this insignia was issued to Belgian volunteers in the Army from 1941 to 1943, it is not seen on 1945 photographs. However it seems unlikely that the new badge designed for SS foreign volunteers ever reached this particular unit.

The 1944 Pattern tunic is cut in woolen olive green cloth. The garment does up with five buttons down the front. The patch pockets have straight edged flaps. The cuff vents close with two buttons each.
Lined with off-white cotton down the front, the tunic has inner pockets. The metal buttons are painted field gray.
A veteran from the Caucasus campaign, the Belgian volunteer wears on his right sleeve the 'edelweiss' badge of the mountain troops. This is woven in silver gray and golden yellow thread on an oval patch. The rank insignia, a star on a round black patch, and the eagle are stitched to the left arm. Both are woven in silver gray thread.

The black leather belt is fitted with a regulation Waffen-SS buckle painted in field gray.
The assault rifle magazine pouches are made of sturdy grayish canvas with dark brown, brown and black leather fittings.
These are suspended from black leather straps.
An egg-shaped grenade hangs from the right chest pocket.

The camouflage trousers are gathered around the ankles. The thick, gray woolen socks are rolled up over the mountain boots and fasten with laces, eyelets and hooks.

Above.
The shoulder straps are piped in white for the infantry. The right collar tab is made of fine black cloth adorned with twin runes woven in white thread. The left collar tab is plain black for private soldiers. The dull silver Infantry Assault Badge is pinned to the left chest pocket.

The trousers are made of close-woven pale yellow cloth. The camouflage consists of brown and green irregular patches overprinted with a thick pattern of small pea green specks. The pattern is repeated every 48 cm. The side slit pockets have buttons. The fob and hip pockets seal with buttons. The fly has six buttons. The button tab arrangements at waist level (two at the front ad two at the back) can be used to fasten either belt or braces. The tapered trouser legs have a drawstring around the bottom edge. The garment adjusts with a buckle strap on both hips. Several patterns of dished metal buttons were used.

The 'Bergmütze' is made of field gray cloth. The turn-up is fastened with two buttons. The death's head on the front and the eagle on the left side are woven in gray thread on a black backing. The regulation Heer edelweiss pinned next to embossed metal eagle was awarded for operations in the Caucasus.

The Waffen-SS 1944 Pattern double-breasted coat was cut in thick, field gray wool and lined with gray material. The eagle and rank insignia are stitched on the left shoulder. The hood is rolled up under the collar and can be kept up with a strap and button arrangement. The coat closes down the front with six buttons. The two chest slit pockets have no flaps.
The sleeves are lined with gray sateen. And inner pocket is provided in the left front. The half belt is fastened with two buttons. Down the lower part of the skirt, the vent flaps overlap and fasten with four synthetic buttons. The other buttons are made of metal and finished in field gray.

The helmet is secured to the belt with its black leather chin strap. In his left hand, the grenadier holds his magazine pouches and suspension straps. The 'Sturmgewehr' (assault rifle) is slung over the right shoulder.

Knitted in gray wool, the gloves stick out of the left slit pocket.

'NEDERLAND' GUNNER, POMERANIA

The parka hood is lowered, showing a green woolen scarf. The officers' belt is fitted with a large, rectangular two-pronged buckle. The black leather holster is used to carry the P-38 pistol. The reversible white/ camouflage parka and trousers are cut in the same cloth. The parka is in mint condition and gives an unfaded portrayal of colors. Padded with wool off-cuts, the double breasted garment is done up with six buttons. The cuffs are fastened with a button and tab arrangement. The drawstring around the waist is made of gray cloth and tightens with a knot. The skirt pockets have slanted openings sealing with pointed buttons flaps.

The baggy trousers are kept up with braces. The fly has four buttons (a set being fitted on both the white and camouflage sides of garment). The leg bottoms are gathered with drawstrings.

The ankle boots are made of black leather.

As early as July 1941, Dutch volunteers flocked to join the ranks of the Waffen SS and fought alongside them on the Eastern Front. On 22 October 1943, the original 'Nederland Freiwilligen Legion' ('Nederland' Volunteer Legion) was expanded into the 'Nederland' 4th SS Panzer Grenadier Brigade before becoming the 'Nederland' 23rd Freiwilligen Panzer Grenadier Division on 10¾February 1945. Dutch volunteers undoubtedly ranked among the most pugnacious soldiers and were therefore frequently deployed in the most exposed sectors of the front. Many of them were awarded the Third Reich's most prestigious decorations. This artillery 'Untersturmführer' is depicted while commissioned with 3rd Panzer Army in Pomerania.

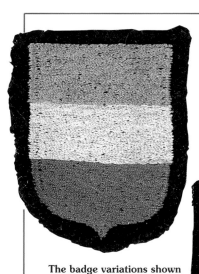
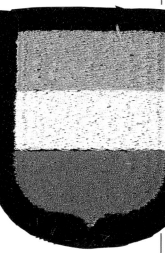

The badge variations shown here were issued to all ranks. Both are late style German manufactured items. The Dutch national colors are displayed horizontally across a shield outlined in black.

Cut in the same Italian cloth as the garments worn by the soldier at right, the 1943 Pattern 'Feldmütze' is piped in silver thread (against regulations as the cap should have had the same white piping as the officer's 'Schirmmütze,' a directive which tended to be rather loosely enforced). The death's head is woven in dull gray thread, while the eagle is rendered in bright silver material. The turn-up is kept up with a synthetic button. The lining is made of green sateen. The cap has no sweat band.

Nederland

Manufactured by BeVo of Wüppertal, the cuff title's lettering and piping are woven in dull gray artificial silk. This pattern was issued to all ranks.

On its obverse, the Waffen-SS officers' regulation buckle bears the 'OLC' trademark in a lozenge (Overhoff & Cie of Lüdenscheid). Made of a zinc and aluminum alloy, it is finished in dull silver.
The buckle depicts an eagle clutching in its talons a wreath adorned with a swastika in the middle. The SS motto 'Meine Ehre heißt Treue' ("My honor is called loyalty") is engraved around the lower edge.

The officers' collar patches are made of black cloth piped with thin aluminum cord. The left patch is adorned with the SS runes, and the right one features the three silver stars (smaller pattern) of a second-lieutenant. The shoulder straps are secured with a loop on the armhole seam and a button near the collar. Made of black cloth with red piping (the artillery branch color) the tabs are adorned with a double interwoven silver braid. The eagle is woven in silver gray thread on a black underlay. The shield is worn above the 'Nederland' cuff title stitched 14.5cm above the lower edge of the cuff.

The Iron Cross 1st Class and a ribbon bar for the Iron Cross 2nd Class and the 1941-42 Russian Campaign Medal are pinned to the left side of the chest. The P-38 pistol holster (early type) is fastened to the soft leather belt.

All the pockets of the 1944 Pattern trousers have button flaps. The leg bottoms are secured with drawstrings. The ankle boots are made of black leather.

'NORDLAND' GUNNER, POMERANIA

After pulling out of Courland, the 'Nordland' SS Panzer Grenadier Division was deployed in Pomerania to defend the borders of the Reich.

There, Scandinavian volunteers were committed alongside Dutch, Flemish, Walloon and German Waffen-SS in a desperate struggle to stem the Russian tide. On 14 February 1944, Operation 'Solstice' was launched but got bogged down after 48 hours' desperate fighting. In this action, the 'Panzerjäger' (tank destroyers) of 'Nordland' occupied Ridge 107 to the south of Hassendorf. The men of Sturmbannführer (major) Schulz-Streek had destroyed no fewer than 22 T-34s when they were forced out of their position.

Below.
1943 Pattern cuff title, manufactured by BeVo of Wüppertal-Barmen, embroidered with black and light gray artificial silk.

Made of black cloth, the WO's shoulder straps are piped in pink, the service color of 'Panzerjägerabteilung 11' (tank destroyer unit). The anti-tank unit's gothic 'P' is made of embossed metal secured with two pins.
The parallelogram-shaped collar patches are made of black cloth piped with a thin silver braid. The two runic 'S' of the 'Schultzstaffel' on the right patch are embroidered in white thread.

The 1943 Pattern 'Feldmütze' (field cap) is cut in low grade, field gray cloth. The turn-up is kept up with a pressed cardboard button. The eagle and the national insignia are woven in dull gray thread on a common trapezoidal light green backing. A black tie is worn with the gray jersey shirt.

The short jacket for tank destroyer crews is cut in the same material as the cap. The soft cloth shows white streaks in places due to the poor quality of the dye. The double-breasted jacket is lined with light tan cotton. It closes with seven dished metal buttons on the right side, the four lower being fly-fronted.

The 'Oberscharführer's (warrant officer) rank is indicated by the two embossed metal stars on the left collar tab. The SS eagle is stitched on the left sleeve. The cuff title is worn 14.5 cm above the lower edge of the cuff. The ribbons for the Iron Cross 2nd Class and the 1941-42 Russian Winter Campaign are stitched through the second buttonhole down the front.

Pinned to the left side of the chest, the 'Nahkampfspange des Heeres' (Infantry Close Combat Clasp) was awarded for 30 days duty involving-hand to hand fighting.

The Iron Cross 1st class and the General Assault Badge are pinned under the clasp.

The buckle fitted to the black regulation belt was on a regular issue to SS personnel up to the rank of 'Sturmscharführer' 'warrant officer with 12 years service).

The black leather holster is for a P-08 pistol. Our man holds a map in his left hand.

Regulation other ranks' sleeve eagle,
embroidered in dull gray thread on a black underlay.

Above, top.
Detail of the fur bonnet: initially meant for the 'Schirmmütze' peaked cap, the SS regulation eagle and death's head pinned to the front of the headgear are stamped in fine zinc. These insignia are either secured with two pins or stitched on (particularly the death's head).

Above.
The other rank's steel belt buckle is finished in pale green. The SS motto "*Meine Ehre heißt Treue*" is engraved in gothic lettering around a central motif showing a spread eagle clutching a swastika girded with an oak leaf wreath.

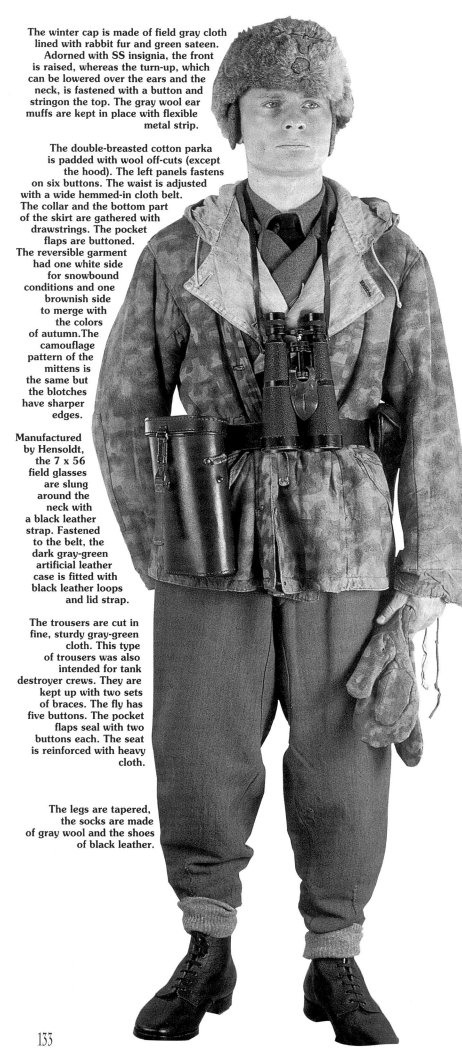

The winter cap is made of field gray cloth lined with rabbit fur and green sateen. Adorned with SS insignia, the front is raised, whereas the turn-up, which can be lowered over the ears and the neck, is fastened with a button and string on the top. The gray wool ear muffs are kept in place with flexible metal strip.

The double-breasted cotton parka is padded with wool off-cuts (except the hood). The left panels fastens on six buttons. The waist is adjusted with a wide hemmed-in cloth belt. The collar and the bottom part of the skirt are gathered with drawstrings. The pocket flaps are buttoned. The reversible garment had one white side for snowbound conditions and one brownish side to merge with the colors of autumn. The camouflage pattern of the mittens is the same but the blotches have sharper edges.

Manufactured by Hensoldt, the 7 x 56 field glasses are slung around the neck with a black leather strap. Fastened to the belt, the dark gray-green artificial leather case is fitted with black leather loops and lid strap.

The trousers are cut in fine, sturdy gray-green cloth. This type of trousers was also intended for tank destroyer crews. They are kept up with two sets of braces. The fly has five buttons. The pocket flaps seal with two buttons each. The seat is reinforced with heavy cloth.

The legs are tapered, the socks are made of gray wool and the shoes of black leather.

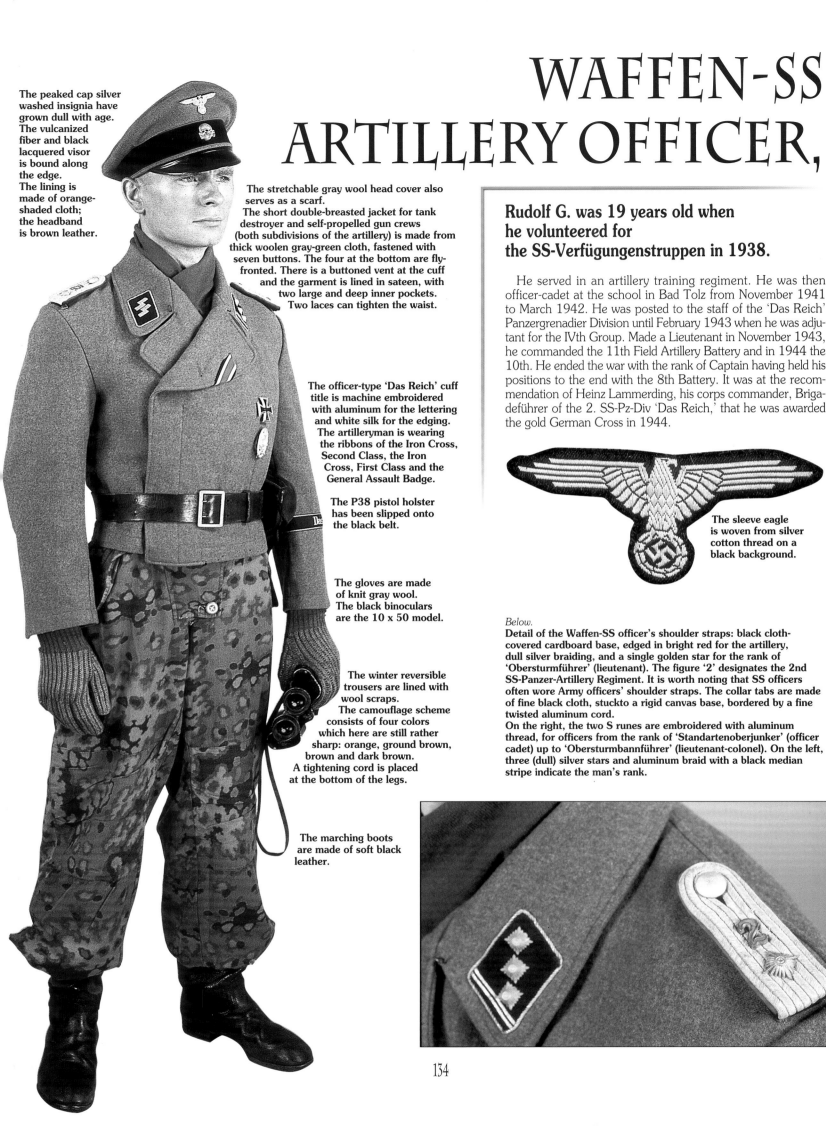

The peaked cap silver washed insignia have grown dull with age. The vulcanized fiber and black lacquered visor is bound along the edge. The lining is made of orange-shaded cloth; the headband is brown leather.

The stretchable gray wool head cover also serves as a scarf.

The short double-breasted jacket for tank destroyer and self-propelled gun crews (both subdivisions of the artillery) is made from thick woolen gray-green cloth, fastened with seven buttons. The four at the bottom are fly-fronted. There is a buttoned vent at the cuff and the garment is lined in sateen, with two large and deep inner pockets. Two laces can tighten the waist.

The officer-type 'Das Reich' cuff title is machine embroidered with aluminum for the lettering and white silk for the edging. The artilleryman is wearing the ribbons of the Iron Cross, Second Class, the Iron Cross, First Class and the General Assault Badge.

The P38 pistol holster has been slipped onto the black belt.

The gloves are made of knit gray wool. The black binoculars are the 10 x 50 model.

The winter reversible trousers are lined with wool scraps. The camouflage scheme consists of four colors which here are still rather sharp: orange, ground brown, brown and dark brown. A tightening cord is placed at the bottom of the legs.

The marching boots are made of soft black leather.

Rudolf G. was 19 years old when he volunteered for the SS-Verfügungenstruppen in 1938.

He served in an artillery training regiment. He was then officer-cadet at the school in Bad Tolz from November 1941 to March 1942. He was posted to the staff of the 'Das Reich' Panzergrenadier Division until February 1943 when he was adjutant for the IVth Group. Made a Lieutenant in November 1943, he commanded the 11th Field Artillery Battery and in 1944 the 10th. He ended the war with the rank of Captain having held his positions to the end with the 8th Battery. It was at the recommendation of Heinz Lammerding, his corps commander, Brigadeführer of the 2. SS-Pz-Div 'Das Reich,' that he was awarded the gold German Cross in 1944.

The sleeve eagle is woven from silver cotton thread on a black background.

Below.
Detail of the Waffen-SS officer's shoulder straps: black cloth-covered cardboard base, edged in bright red for the artillery, dull silver braiding, and a single golden star for the rank of 'Obersturmführer' (lieutenant). The figure '2' designates the 2nd SS-Panzer-Artillery Regiment. It is worth noting that SS officers often wore Army officers' shoulder straps. The collar tabs are made of fine black cloth, stuck to a rigid canvas base, bordered by a fine twisted aluminum cord.
On the right, the two S runes are embroidered with aluminum thread, for officers from the rank of 'Standartenoberjunker' (officer cadet) up to 'Obersturmbannführer' (lieutenant-colonel). On the left, three (dull) silver stars and aluminum braid with a black median stripe indicate the man's rank.